REFLECTIONS AND MEDITATIONS ON THE SIGNS OF THE ZODIAC

LOUISE HUBER

Translated by Moray Patterson

First published in German in 1981 by Verlag Astrologisch-Psychologisches Institut, Switzerland under the title *Die Tierkreiszeichen - Reflexionen Meditationen.*

First Printing 1984
Second Printing 1990
ISBN Number: 0-86690-272-4
Library of Congress Number: 83-73610

Cover Design: E. Bruggmann, Michael A. Huber
Graphic Design: Michael A. Huber

Published by:
American Federation of Astrologers, Inc.
P.O. Box 22040, 6535 South Rural Road
Tempe, Arizona 85285-2040

Printed in the United States of America

Reflections and Meditations On The Signs of The Zodiac

New insights into the background of the twelve signs of the Zodiac. The spiritual path and crises of transformation of each individual sign. Selected texts for Full Moon meditations.

Table of Contents

Planet — Symbol

Sun	☉	♂	Mars
Moon	☾	♃	Jupiter
Saturn	♄	♅	Uranus
Mercury	☿	♆	Neptune
Venus	♀	♇	Pluto
North Node of the Moon	☊		

Zodiac — Symbol

Aries	♈	♎	Libra
Taurus	♉	♏	Scorpio
Gemini	♊	♐	Sagittarius
Cancer	♋	♑	Capricorn
Leo	♌	♒	Aquarius
Virgo	♍	♓	Pisces

Preface

Dear Reader,

In the course of centuries much has been written about astrology, and in particular about the signs of the Zodiac. In this book I do not wish to repeat what you can read in every other book on astrology. My purpose is to suggest to you a new perspective and to comment on the psychological effects, crises of transformation and the spiritual path which everyone must run according to the sign of the Zodiac under which he is born.

I wish to develop the theme of the signs of the Zodiac more from the point of view of development and evolution and to lay the main emphasis on the esoteric content. In order to make this intelligible, I should like to introduce three points right at the start.

1. Beside its well-known cosmic influences on our planet the annual movement of the Sun through the twelve signs of the Zodiac has a special relationship to the spiritual development of a human being. Everyone can receive the cosmic energies which flow into our planet during this cycle and use them for the benefit of his own spiritual and personal development. This means that you will be able to attune yourself consciously to specific signs of the Zodiac even if you are not born under the sign in question.

2. According to ancient tradition a transmission of energy has been taking place on the spiritual plane since time immemorial every month at the time of the Full Moon, which has a special effect, in accordance with the sign of the Zodiac in which the Sun is situated at the time, on the development of Mankind. You can tune in through meditation, either alone or in a group, to this flow of energy. The energies which you have received in this way will revitalize your will for life, bring about the changes and transformations necessary for your development and will flow on through you to all humanity.

3. In the Age of Aquarius the Full Moon Meditations shall become the most important monthly festivals of the "New World Religion". Therefore, each of us is called upon today to concern himself with them. It would be a good thing if everywhere in the world groups were formed which could facilitate through communal meditation the flowing in of spiritual energies so that the way may be prepared for that which is to come.

Meditation groups already exist throughout the whole world which meditate every month at the time of the Full Moon. In some of these groups the Zodiac texts which are to be found in this book are used. These serve to accustom you intellectually to the special qualities of the signs. A mental aura is thus created which, besides its calming and inspiring effect, facilitates the transmission of energy.

I have written this book in thankful memory to Roberto Assagioli, the founder of Psychosynthesis and the precursor of Transpersonal Psychology. I had the privilege of being his secretary in Florence for three years. In daily communal meditation he helped me greatly to become aware of my own inspirations and to write them down and to interpret them. I have worked for twenty years on the texts of the twelve signs of the Zodiac and every year during the period of the Full Moon new realizations about the individual signs came to me. Over the coming years I could and more in the monthly cycle, but one must stop at some time and pass on what one has in one's heart. Many revelations are still to come to us, and I am certain that many will come after me who will discover and write down more about the flowing in of spiritual energies to our planet.

Therefore, I hope that this book about the signs of the Zodiac will induce you too during the period of the Full Moon—when you can see the Moon shining fully in the sky—to open yourself to the special qualities of the Zodiac or to meditate communally on them in a group.

Switzerland, Fall 1980 Louise Huber

THE EARTH AND THE ZODIAC

Three Approaches • The energy aspect of the earth •
Astrology: A subjective, geocentric view of the world •
The relationship of the zodiac to the constellations of the fixed stars •
Zodiac and constellations (drawing) • The zodiac—
a projection of human feeling and thinking •
The twelve archetypes • The earth as a great living body. •
The "Aura of the earth"—early forms of astrology •
The magnetic mantel of the earth, the latest scientific insights •

The zodiac—"The House System of our planet" •
Types of relationships •
The etherical body of our planet, the subtle energy of light •
Reflexion and Meditation on the Planetary Logos •
Exercise in Meditation •

Three Approaches

For a better understanding of the signs of the Zodiac we must form a clear idea of what these actually are, of the way in which they affect us and of how we can use their influences in our development.

We can go about this in three different ways. First, from the scientific point of view, secondly, through intuitive experience or sensory perception, and thirdly, through spiritual expansion into cosmic analogies—into the Universal Consciousness.

The first approach to the signs of the Zodiac is concerned with physical reality, with the perception through our concrete mind of our planet Earth embedded in cosmic space and in the Zodiac.

The second approach is a question of mantic-magical experience as Early Man was still capable of experiencing and which we are able to develop again today with the help of psychological reasoning, with the ability to perceive through our senses and with mediation. In this way the intellect becomes receptive to intuitive impressions as a bridge is built from concrete to abstract understanding, from the intellect to intuition.

The third approach is primarily an abstract or esoteric examination and a symbolic representation of the Whole with which we identify. This causes an expansion of our consciousness into cosmic realms and relationships, a respectful understanding of the greatness of creation, of which we recognize ourselves to be a part.

The Energy Aspect of the Earth

What do we mean when we talk about the "energy aspect" of the Earth? In astrology almost exclusive consideration is given to the influences of planets, signs and houses, but little is said about the Earth as a planet, although the Earth with its living creatures emits such dynamic rays that we must not overlook them. Our Earth is no dead body, it has a highly dynamic life-principle which we may call the "energy aspect" of our planet. It is the "Spirit of the Earth" in its totality, the energy and radiation of the whole of nature.

All physical and spiritual life on our planet is a manifestation of energy. This fact is easily forgotten, although the whole of astrological knowledge, and in fact of life itself, is based on energy and radiation.

Today astrologers talk about symbolism, psychic functions, planetary rays, karma, synchronicity, Fate and Free Will, but little is said about energy as the basis of all astrological phenomena.

In other fields of research into human beings, like psychology and parapsychology, we are beginning to look on the human organism and its psyche as an energy pattern of specific energies which can be blocked or which can flow freely in all directions. Psychotherapeutic techniques, such as psychosynthesis, Gestallt therapy, concentrate on mobilizing an individual's own energies and integrating these energies into a functional whole.

If we want to form an idea of our Earth, of its radiation out into Space and of its effects on our own lives, then we must likewise learn to think in terms of energy. If, for example, we open ourselves inwardly in our experience of nature or in meditation, we soon realize that we are continually surrounded by different kinds of energy vibrations about which we have no idea in the hustle and bustle of everyday life. We can feel how we are embedded in a continuously moving energy field which affects us, animates us or weakens us according to our disposition and according to the way in which we react to such influences. It is important to know something about the effects of this energy because we can then adjust ourselves to it better. In this respect we are helped both by astrology, as the ancient science of human beings, as well as by a meditative approach to the qualities of the Zodiac.

This energy field in which we live is influenced not only by the rays emitted by our planet Earth and by the incoming rays from cosmic forces but also by the many people around us. In order to develop this idea, I should like you to imagine that our Earth is, in a global sense, a living organism and that Mankind, as well as the animal, plant and mineral kingdoms, are all forms of expression of this great Being. In esoteric texts this entity is called the "Planetary Logos", the "Ancient of Days" or "Sanat Kumara". It is the Spirit of the Earth, that great Being of which we are unable to form any real image, in which however we live, move and have our being. We are in a constant, living exchange with Him, taking our part in the great energetic movements, in the cyclical processes and in the development of this great Being. From this fact all the great religions of the world have arisen, as well as the idea of the "Divine Father", whose children we are and in whose image we remain, in the sense of "I and the Father are one".

In order to achieve a deeper understanding of the signs of the Zodiac we must turn our thoughts to analogies. "As in the small, so in the large" runs an old saying. Just as the system of houses in our individual horoscope represents the place and the environment into which we are born, so the twelve divisions of the celestial sphere or Zodiac surrounding the Earth are nothing more nor less than the cosmic environment within which life on Earth runs its course. We are therefore nothing more than the *microcosm of the macrocosm*.

Moreover, with the assistance of analogy we can imagine how our planet is constructed in the same way as ourselves. If we think for a moment of our horoscope: in the center of the circle is our Self around which the planets with their mutual aspects are arranged, the Zodiac and the houses too.

If we imagine by way of analogy the Earth as a globe in the middle of a horoscope, as shown in the drawing on page 5 then the twelve houses of Man correspond to the twelve signs of the Zodiac of the "Planetary Logos". The ancients had already called the signs of the Zodiac the "heavenly houses" in which the Sun, in the course of the twelve months of the year, dwelt one after the other.

We make a distinction therefore between the constellations far out in space and our belt of the Zodiac around the Earth which represents the path of the Sun. Even Ptolomaeus of Alexandria, who brought together the observations and insights of the Babylonian astrologers in his "Tetrabiblos", made a strict distinction between these two Zodiacs, basing astrological thought on the solar Zodiac, that is to say, *our* Zodiac.

Astrology: A Subjective, Geocentric View Of The World

If we want to gain a true picture of the astrological way of thinking, and of the theme of this book, that is, of the Zodiac, then we must bear in mind that astrology looks at the cosmos from the point of view of the planet Earth. It is not based on the Copernican view of the world, but on the earlier Ptolomaic one according to which the Earth was situated at the center of all cosmic activity. If we look at the night sky, then we can see the heavenly sphere with all its stars slowly moving in a clockwise direction.

We cannot see the Zodiac with the naked eye, but we can picture it as a broad band drawn across the sky through which the Sun appears to travel as it moves in the course of a year along the ecliptic, and in which the Moon and the planets also appear to move. We call this "apparent" motion because we are in fact dealing here with a subjective way of looking at things; that is, from a purely astronomical point of view the Sun is the center of all motion, whereas from an astrological point of view everything is seen from the Earth.

In the final analysis astrology is not about the stars but about people who live on the Earth, and about their embeddedness in the Cosmic Whole. For that reason, from an astrological point of view, the Cosmos must be described in the way in which Man actually sees it.

In order to give you an idea of what the Zodiac looks like in astronomy, I should like to show you a drawing.

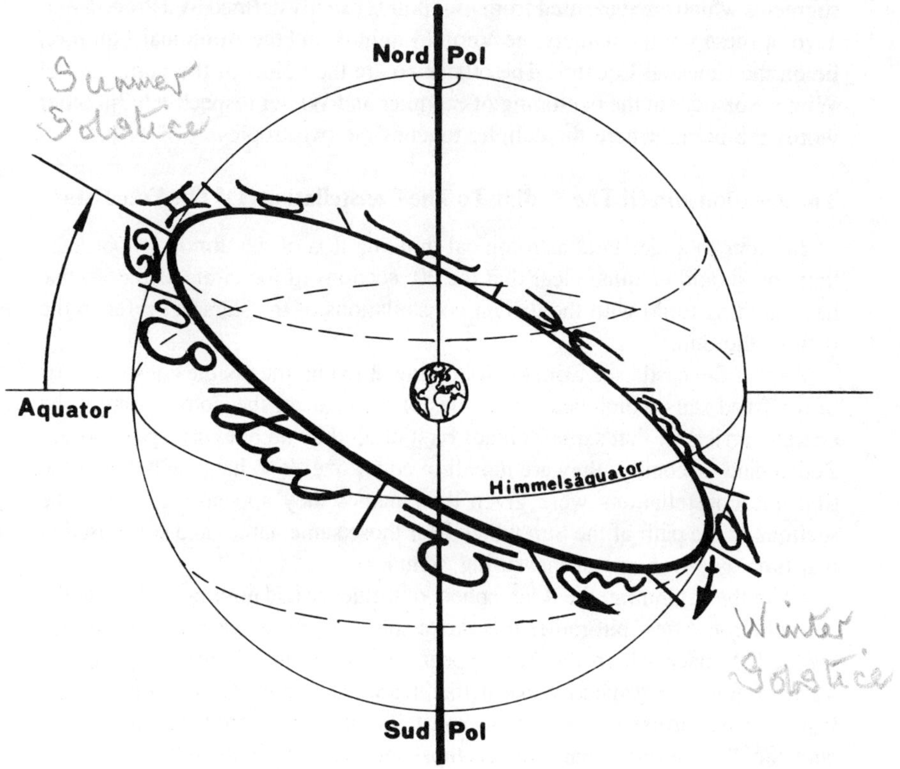

The vertical axis passes through the celestial North Pole, at which the Pole Star is situated, and through the South Pole. Between the two the equator runs round the Earth. The two inner circles represent the Celestial Equator and the Tropics of Cancer and Capricorn. At an angle to these you see the ecliptic, the band of the Zodiac through which the Sun passes in the course of a year from the 21st March to the 20th March of the following year.

As you can see, the ecliptic lies at an angle because the axis of the Earth is inclined at an angle of 23°27′. In one half of the year it inclines to the north and in the other half to the south. This causes the seasons and is the reason why we have longer days in Summer and shorter days in Winter.

The Zodiac represents an equal division of the ecliptic into twelve 30° segments which are measured from four points exactly defined by astronomers. Two of these points, namely the Vernal Equinox and the Autumnal Equinox, lie on the Celestial Equator. The other two are the points of the Summer and Winter Solstices at the beginning of Summer and Winter respectively; in other words the points where the ecliptic touches the two tropics.

The Relationship Of The Zodiac To The Constellations Of The Fixed Stars

In order to understand astrological thinking it is of the utmost importance that you should be quite clear that the 30° sections of the circle of the Zodiac have nothing to do with the distant constellations of the stars but refer to the path of the Sun.

As you can easily see from the following drawing, the visible constellations of the fixed stars which bear the names of the signs of the Zodiac are not the energy carriers of that same Zodiac. First of all they do not correspond to our Zodiac and, secondly, they are not all of equal size. It so happened that at the time the constellations were given their names they appeared to cover the sections of the path of the Sun which bear those same names and were used at that time as astronomical measuring points.

From the beginning, the Aries sphere of influence had nothing to do with the constellation Aries; but rather this Aries sphere of influence was, and is still today, the space which the Sun appears to move through after passing the Vernal Equinox, irrespective of whether it is actually in the constellation Aries, Pisces or Aquarius. It is not these constellations which emit the energies in question, but the signs; that is to say, those sections of the path of the Sun which at the moment lie some 30° to the right of the constellations with the same names. This also refutes the attacks of astronomers that the signs of the Zodiac no longer agree with the constellations of the fixed stars, but have moved on in accordance with the Procession of the Equinoxes.

By way of a more exact illustration of this fact I have reproduced a drawing by Bruno Huber.

Explanation of the Drawing

The outer sections show the extent of each constellation. The numbers on the outer circle indicate the number of years which the equinox takes to pass through the corresponding constellation.

The dates shown on the edges of the sectors indicate respectively the beginning and the ending of the Procession of the Equinox through a constellation.

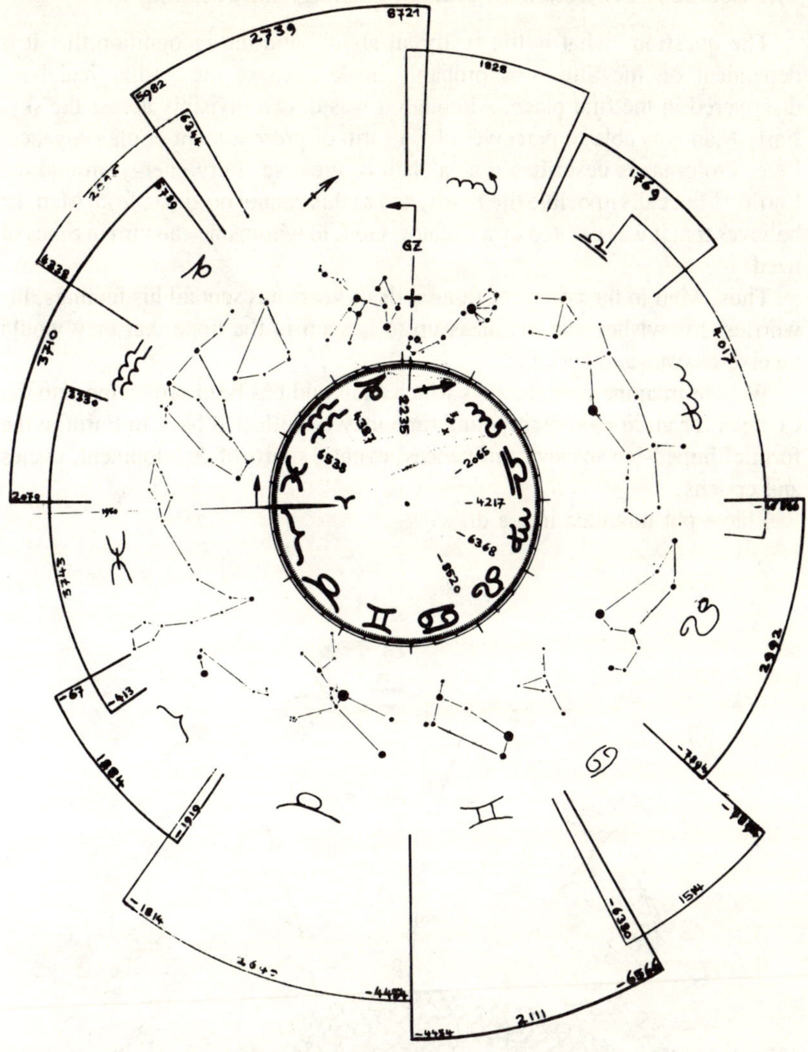

Zodiac and Constellation

The Zodiac-A Projection Of Human Feeling And Thinking

The question "what is life really all about" and the recognition that it is dependent on the Sun, was probably made because the Zodiac had been discovered in the first place. Although it was drawn invisibly across the sky, Early Man was able to perceive it by a form of presentiment or clairvoyance. Later Ptolomaeus described it as a "belt of creative, fiery energy around the Earth". Man calls invisible life Spirit, and as this cannot originate from Man, he believes that it was created by a Creator, God, to whom one can turn in times of need.

Thus, Man in the course of thousands of years has sent all his feelings, his worries, his wishes and his ideas up to heaven in the hope that they would receive answer and succour.

We can imagine how the rays which Mankind has been projecting into the Cosmos for an immemorably long time may be reflected back to Earth in the form of hoped-for answers, influences, events, spurts of development, cycles and epochs.

I have put this idea into a drawing.

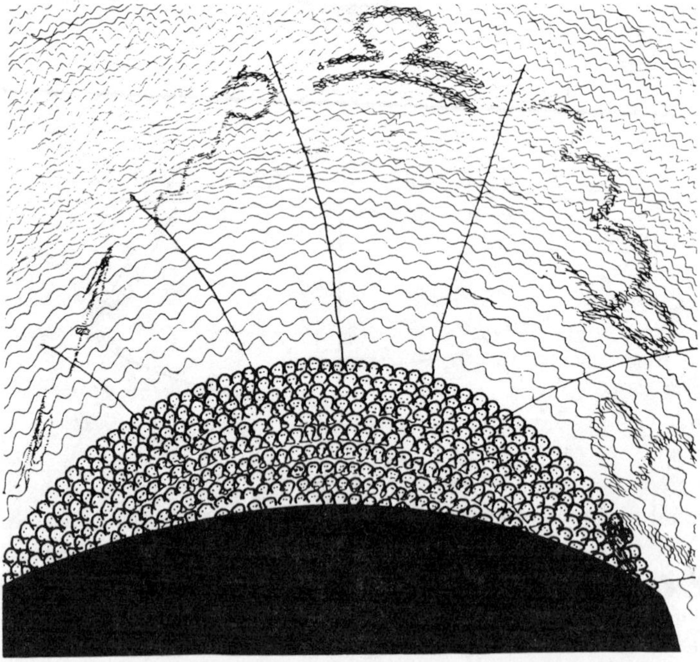

Looked at in this way, the ideas, wishes and thought forms of Man create out there in the space surrounding the Earth various pictures which we can call the Zodiac. It is a pulsating process of the emission and reception of rays, of coming and going, of *invocation and evocation*, or of aspiration which calls forth a response.

The qualities of the signs of the Zodiac and the planetary energies have a corresponding effect in their turn on the Earth and on her living creatures. The division of the belt of the Zodiac into twelve parts does not derive therefore from the sky above, but from the imagination of Mankind. One can even go so far as to accept that all the energies in the Cosmos are present in each individual human being—who is thus only a mirror image of the Cosmos. The Zodiac is so full of cultural layers that it is impossible to ever describe it exhaustively.

In the view of *esoteric science* it is out of this hierarchy that the planetary astral level developed, which in reality does not represent a cosmic principle but which has been created by Man himself in the course of aeons and which, among other things, manifests itself in the effects of the twelve signs of the Zodiac. From the spiritual stand point astrology therefore rests on illusions: not only because the Zodiac is the imaginary path of the Sun across the sky, but because of the power of projection and imagination of Mankind. From this point of view the Zodiac is a projection of human feeling and thought and therefore has an effect in turn on primarily these two functions. Our *spiritual Self* however remains untouched by it and is free of astrological influences.

Nevertheless, the influences of the signs of the Zodiac and of the planets remain real for Mankind and have a demonstrable effect because we human beings live primarily in our psyche and in our thinking and feeling.

The Twelve Archetypes

In psychology archetypes are primeval images which are active in the Collective Unconscious and which largely determine human behaviour. These primeval images can also be looked on as the agglomeration of unconscious energies possessing a common structure. They have an effect on those individuals who have become sensitive to them and who show a similar make-up.

Modern astrology has come to recognize that the components of astrology, above all the signs of the Zodiac and the planets, also have an archetypal character. It has been proved that people whose Sun is situated in the same sign, that is to say, people who are born in the same month, react in many matters in the same manner. The archetypal part of the sun in question shows the same characteristics.

Carl Gustav Jung describes the archetypal effects of the Collective Unconscious in a way which we can transfer without further qualification to the twelve signs of the Zodiac and also to the symbolic contents of the planetary energies. He says:

> The Collective Unconscious is the psychic primal reality, the reservoir of basic motifs and primal forms common to Man, of the archetypes of life. It is not instinctual but symbolic. It is the home of the creative imagination of the Spirit and of one's feeling of value which cannot be shaken by reason. The Unconscious, together with the Conscious and the area of the Superpersonal, form a common field of social relationships and ethical values within which nothing can occur which does not have an influence on all parts of the field.

Thus, it becomes clear that all life consists fundamentally of a single homogeneous substance, of energy which binds all of us to one another. We can only have this experience when we consciously thrust into the deepest layers of our Being, to which end astrological psychology, that is, sensual perception, as well as personal, meditative experience serves. This conception of the living and of the organic in the world should come first in every observation and in every meditation which an individual makes. In this way we are led on from unity to detail, from the whole to the individual, from the great to the small, and not the other way around. In nature we always notice first of all the wood and then the trees, the meadow and then the grass, first of all the appearance of the whole individual and only then the traits of his character.

In astrological-psychological interpretation the Whole, the unity, has a greater significance than the sum of its parts which are brought together by the formalistic and analytical intellect. Therefore, sensory experience, the immersion in the reality of life, is the right approach for the comprehension of astrological and spiritual relationships.

The Earth As A Great Living Body

In this sense we can also imagine the Earth as a great living body in which humanity as a living organism, divided into single cells or group cells, moves and has its Being. The make-up of all living organisms is the same; as is known, our body consists of many cells and in the same way we are a cell in the body of our "Planetary Logos". This is yet again a cell within a still larger Being, the Solar Logos, and so on. Dane Rudhyar described this state in his book "Astrology of The Personality" in an impressive way. Similarly Johannes Kepler in his book the "Harmony of the Spheres".

Thus, one system depends on another: our human organism on the planetary organism, this in turn on the Solar System, which is a part of further and still larger systems, up to the Galactic System, whose organism or body is a complete spiral cloud.

It is worthwhile to imagine the magnitudes involved here, for then we get an idea of cosmic laws which we can transfer to our own small lives. Even the great astronomer Kepler did not consider the Earth as a purely mathematical heavenly body but as a great organism. Thus, he writes in his book "Harmonices Mundi":

> The whole of creation forms a wonderful symphony in the arrangement of the mind and of the spirit, as well as in the physical world. Everything is sustained by and connected through mutual, indissoluable relationships, a harmonious Whole is formed. Everything that exists is animated and full of life, because all things are mutually connected and bound up. There is no star which is not a living Being, which does not possess a Soul. The Souls of the stars are the cause of their movements and their attractions, uniting the stars one to another. It explains the regularity of natural phenomena.

The "Aura Of The Earth"—Early Forms Of Astrology

The great field of relationships between all living things on the Earth can also be imagined as an "aura", as a large radiating field of the whole of the race of Man and, seen in a larger context, as the field of relationships between the Cosmos and the Earth.

The idea of the Earth having the Zodiac as its aura was certainly in existence in the Middle Ages. One could not comprehend it as something physical; it is a typically occult, mystical definition. Looked at in this way the Zodiac, or the Aura of the Earth is a sphere of swirling energies in which Mankind and the Cosmos find immaterial contact. In order to understand this and to be able to appreciate it, we must of course free ourselves from the objective intellect and identify ourselves with this idea in contemplative and meditative experience.

In this respect it is advantageous to return to the point of departure, to those beginnings in the dawn of time when Mankind did not comprehend nature through his understanding but experienced it in contemplation. This is in complete contrast to our present-day technological age in which everything is measured by the concrete and in which the calculating intellect finds with ease constructions and definitions which have nothing to do with real life. It is necessary to bear living processes in mind, to return to the observation of nature and to the perception of real life-processes so that we may experience the origin of life again.

For example, when we look at the splendour of the starlit night sky then we are filled with awe and wonder. We are lifted up out of the cares of our daily life and can take part in a greater world. Man has always seen something incomprehensible in the starlit sky, an iron order and regularity which sustains and regulates life. Early cultural Man considered nothing to be caused; all events which transcended limited understanding were ascribed to forces of nature or to gods.

Human beings were in direct contact with nature, they had to come to terms with her, they were exposed to her and had to find ways and means of protecting themselves or of gaining the goodwill of the gods through worship and sacrifice. We in the West today live in a world which is protected on all sides and we have little access to nature. Therefore, it is important for us to return to the point of departure so as to rediscover the threads of genuine experience. Astrology arose in the first place out of the relationship between Man and nature or supposed gods, and the astrological way of thinking can only be correctly understood from this point of view.

Ptolemaeus was correct when he saw the Zodiac as a ring of fire around the Earth, for today science is almost on the point of discovering it to be just that, just as psychology has discovered that the fundamental astrological symbols are generally valid human stereotypes and that they belong to the archetypes of the Collective Unconscious.

The Magnetic Mantle Of The Earth
The Latest Scientific Insights

At the present time we are in a position to say what this Earth-Aura is. It can be equated with the magnetic mantle which surrounds the Earth. In the course of the investigation of outer space a magnetic band of radiation around the Earth with its various layers was discovered. Recently it was further discovered that a continuously changing gravitational configuration arises through the structure of the momentary movements of the planets in the Solar System. Every body in the Solar System has its own gravitational field. The Sun has the strongest and can hold all the other planets together. The gravitational fields of the planets taken together produce a common gravitational configuration, a large gravitational field in the Solar System, which is continuously changing because the planets are always moving carrying their fields with them.

Astrology does nothing more than register the effect of these continuously changing magnetic fields on the magnetic field of the Earth and attempts to record and demonstrate them through the aspects in every individual horoscope; aspects and angular relations to the planets as seen from the Earth have always been recognized since time immemorial as having an effect. However, what is really being measured is the condition of the energies of the terrestrial magnetic field influenced by the gravitational effects which emanate from the visible planets of our Solar System.

In biological research as well it was recently discovered for example that bees and even migratory birds can orientate themselves according to the magnetic rays of the Earth and the Sun. A lot of research must still be done here, but it is obvious to us that this terrestrial magnetic mantle is connected with the twelve signs of the Zodiac and that the planets which move within it cause astrological effects which we can ascertain in the horoscopes of individual people and of the whole of Mankind.

The Zodiac—"The House System Of Our Planet"

If we understand the Zodiac to be a ring around the Earth, then it is relatively easy to look on it as the system of houses of our planet (see diagram).

As we have already explained exhaustively in our book, "Man And His World", the individual twelve houses are built up around humanity to whose aura and living space they belong, and constitute the field which sensitizes him to his surroundings.

The Earth moves through the Solar System just as an individual moves through his surroundings, with which he is in contact through the system of houses. The Zodiac, as the magnetic field of our Earth, is accordingly "the cosmic environment" of the Earth and thus the "system of houses of the planet" which is divided into twelve signs or areas equal to them in size.

Through these the Earth is connected to all extraterrestrial influences as well as to all terrestrial forms of life. All cosmic relationships into which the Earth can enter and which can have an effect on the Earth's atmosphere must pass through the ring of the Zodiac and be colored by it.

All planetary influences which reach the Earth are stamped by the sign of the Zodiac in which they are situated. The planets are supplied as it were with nourishment by the signs and are correspondingly modified.

In astrological-psychological interpretation we also speak of a planet in a personal horoscope as an individual life-energy or as an organism, being imprinted by the sign in which it is placed at the time of birth. Thus the signs indicate one's disposition, what is already present or what has been inherited.

Types Of Relationships

According to the esoteric law "as above, so below" we can establish the following relationships:

The "*individual system of houses*" unites Man with the outer world, as with the inner world.

The "*system of houses of the Earth*", the Zodiac, unites the Earth with the Solar System, as well as with Mankind and the animal and plant kingdoms. The Zodiac unites the individual Being with influences from the Solar System, as well as with all other men. It is a large field of relationships and connections divided into twelve parts not only for humanity but also for the planet Earth.

"*As in the macrocosm, so in the microcosm*", to quote a good thinker.

The Etheric Body Of Our Planet
The Subtle Energy Of Light

Now we come to a more esoteric consideration of this whole theme. You will have already noticed that we must penetrate to a deeper layer of astrological thought in order to discover the hidden meaning of the Zodiac. 'Esoteric' means the arcane, that which lies behind external appearances. Today interest is particularly great in subtle subjects, in light- or life-energies, which can also cause parapsychological phenomena.

From the *esoteric point of view*, which is always a more energy-orientated way of thinking, one speaks of the etheric body of our planet, of a subtle sphere of light which penetrates through all solid things and which animates everything. The ether of space is the field in which and through which the energy of our "Planetary Logos" is effective. It is a large field of cosmic energies in which we live and with which we can come into contact through meditation.

The House System

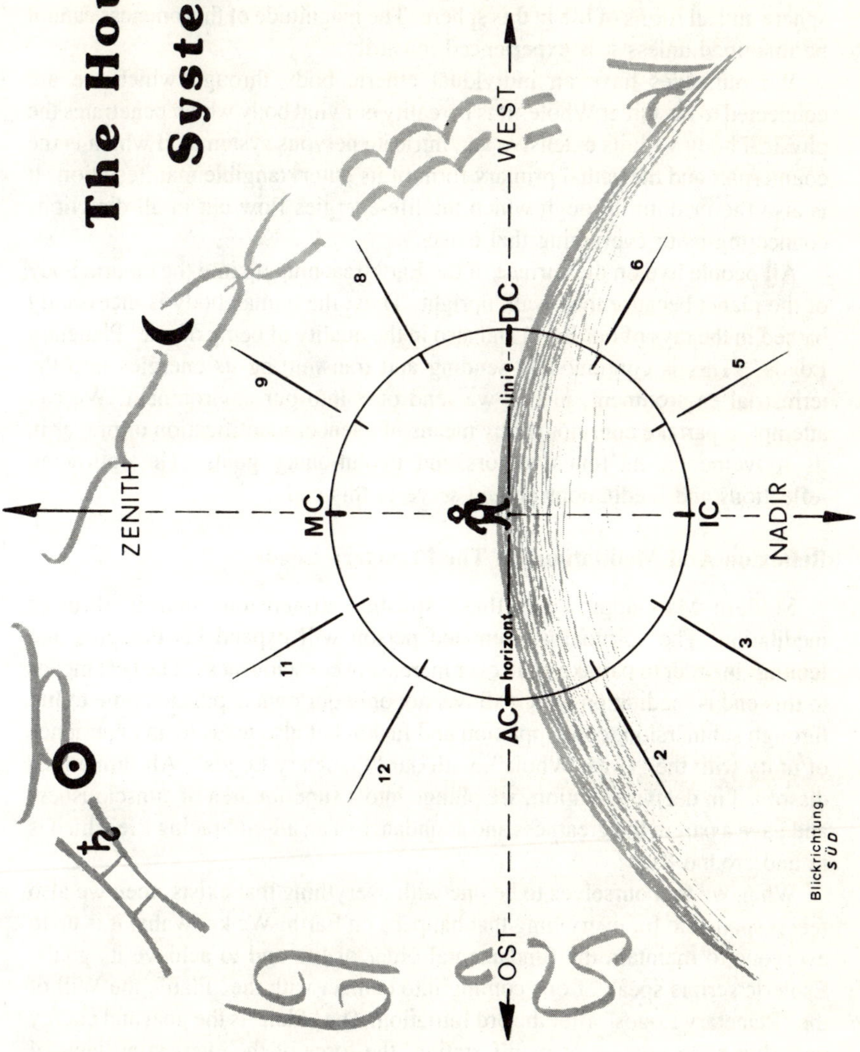

In this respect we are dealing with the etheric body of our planet, of the Solar System and of related planetary systems (stellar families), as well as with the general, gigantic etheric body of the universe in which we live. This huge area, just as the smaller locally restricted fields, is the means of the transmission of all those energies which act on and through our Solar System, our planetary sphere and all forms of life in this sphere. The magnitude of this oneness cannot be imagined unless it is experienced inwardly.

We ourselves have an individual etheric body through which we are connected to the Great Whole. It is in reality our vital body which penetrates the physical body with its extensive and intricate nervous system and which is the counterpart and the actual primary form of its outer, tangible manifestation. It is also the medium through which the life-energies flow out in all directions connecting us to everything that exists.

All people live on the surface of the Earth reaching up into the etheric body of the planet because they walk upright. Thus, the human body is incessantly bathed in the rays of our Earth and also in the quality of being of our "Planetary Logos". This is continuously sending and transmitting its energies into the terrestrial environment, just as we send ours into our environment. We can attempt to partake consciously by means of silence, identification or prayer in its movements, its tones, colors and evolutionary goals. The following reflections and meditations should serve to this end.

Reflexion And Meditation On The Planetary Logos

Modern Man approaches these spiritual dimensions mainly through meditation. The spiritually orientated person will expand his thoughts and feelings in order to partake of an ever increasing consciousness. The best means to this end is meditation which allows not only our own depths to come to life through submersion, contemplation and fusion but also leads to an experience of unity with the "Great Whole", with our "Planetary Logos". All limitations dissolved in deep meditation, we plunge into a superior area of consciousness and have a part in the greatness and abundance of an all-embracing life which is in and around us.

When we feel ourselves to be one with everything that exists, then we also feel responsible for everything that happens on Earth. We know that it is up to everyone to maintain the fundamental order of life and to achieve its goals. Esoteric scripts speak of one coming into contact with the "Plan", the Will of the "Planetary Logos" after the 3rd Initiation. The "Plan" is the goal and energy underlying the process of manifestation, the force of the everlasting laws of development which do not only exist in space and time but which remain in force throughout a far greater cycle and which are adjusted to the goals of evolution. Many call these superior laws the Will of God, conformity to the laws of nature or development, the motivating and impulse-giving energies which radiate from our "Planetary Logos" itself and which flow into our earthly life through the signs of the Zodiac and the planets.

In such processes of consciousness and perception the small personal Self becomes ever less important. We grow beyond the narrow scope of our own personalities and consciously join the life of the Cosmos. We recognize that we are in constant and inextricable contact with all life on our planet and with the whole universe. Thus, everything disappears which torments, worries or disturbs our personal Ego. It is like a homecoming, like being welcomed, a joyous feeling of being uplifted in a greater order and Love which is not of this world, which permeates us, however, with a warmth of safety and security arising from unity and belonging.

Exercise In Meditation

We are sitting comfortably and relaxed in our chairs; we close our eyes and become more and more composed. We loosen all our muscles, we are not holding on to anything. We feel deep into our forehead letting the muscles become quite loose and relaxed. Our forehead becomes smooth, our face friendly, relaxed. Our tongue is placed in the lower jaw, our breath passes calmly and evenly through the nose. We contemplate: "I breathe".

We concentrate on the point between our eyebrows, then we keep the threefold personality (physical, emotional and mental) equally balanced uniting with the Self, the Soul, which dwells within us.

We expand our consciousness and lovingly encompass the whole planet, we feel as one with everything that breathes and lives.

> Oh, Thou in whom we live, breathe and have our being, the power which makes all things new, turn the fate of Men to better things, everywhere move the hearts of Men so that they may open themselves to the spirit of love and brotherhood and mutual responsibility.
>
> May the Will for Good be the motive of all deeds and may it establish once again the reign of peace on Earth.
>
> May the love of the One Life irradiate our hearts, our group and through us the whole world.

We unite with all those people whom we know, we feel united with them through the spirit which we emit to humanity through a joint OM.

OM

SIGNS—MEDITATION

Introduction

Today we hear much about meditation and an increasing number of techniques are offered for a better understanding of ourselves and our lives. Many people wish to come into contact with spiritual energies so as to derive guidance and help from them. I do not wish to offer a new technique of meditation through these Zodiac meditations but to draw your attention to the fact that every month ever newer energies pour into our planet which we can understand consciously and apply in our lives.

Astrology has always concerned itself with Man and his relationship to cosmic energies. The modern direction in astrology of "astrological psychology" discerns the human psyche in the horoscope, its manifold expressions of life, structures of behavior and opportunities for development. Meditation is also concerned with Man, but even more with his spiritual dimension, with his deepest levels of Being, the center of his Being which unites him with everything that lives. "Without meditation a human being cannot really become a human being at all".

In astrological psychology we draw the horoscope with a circle in the middle which symbolizes the innermost Being, the true Self, the center of Man's Being. In astrological interpretation we try to comprehend the outer spaces and influences lying around this circle.

The planets in the signs and houses indicate how Man reacts to his environment; the configuration of aspects reflects states of consciousness, our inner motivations; the signs of the Zodiac indicate the genetic structure, the hereditary factors that a person brings into the world with him, to which the psychic, spiritual characteristics also belong.

The Zodiac provides a cosmic system of reference which brings us into contact with the psychic and spiritual qualities of each sign.

The Zodiac meditations are an attempt at coming into contact in meditation with the *cosmic sources* of the signs of the Zodiac. We can look on the qualities of the signs as ever gushing sources of pure cosmic energy which are actually always at our disposal. Everybody has all twelve of these basic qualities in his horoscope. But each month, especially at the time of the Full Moon, these special qualities flow onto the Earth and onto humanity in greater measure. They do not only influence the mentality of the person born under the sign, that is to say his Sun was placed in that sign at birth, but at the same time also stimulate all life on our planet.

According to ancient tradition a special transmission of energy takes place every month at the time of the Full Moon. In the Zodiac meditations we can tune in directly to this transmission, either alone or as a group, at the Full Moon, on the days before or after.

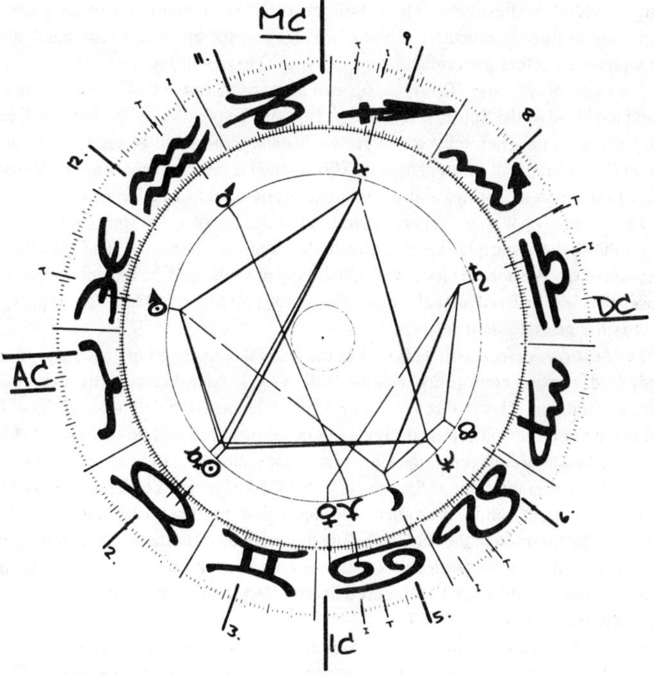

According to Alice A. Bailey the Full Moon meditations shall occupy a special place in the new world religion. On the days of the monthly Full Moons festive hours with ritual actions will be observed, whereby "three great festivals in three successive months will take place . . .". These are the Easter Festival in April, the Wesak Festival in May and the Festival of Goodwill in June.

The Three Full Moon Festivals

Excerpts from Alice A. Bailey's book "The Externalisation Of The Hierarchy" (pages 420–422).

Let me indicate the possibilities of such spiritual events, and prophesy the nature of the coming world-wide Festivals. There will be three such major Festivals each year, concentrated in three consecutive months, and leading therefore to a prolonged spiritual effort which will affect the remainder of the year. These will be:

1. *The Festival of Easter*. This is the festival of the risen, living Christ, the Teacher of all men and the Head of the Spiritual Hierarchy. He is the Expression of the Love of God. On this day the Spiritual Hierarchy which He guides and directs will be recognized, and the nature of God's love will be emphasized. This festival is determined always by the date of the first Full Moon of spring, and is the great Western and Christian festival.

2. *The Festival of Wesak*. This is the festival of the Buddha, the spiritual Intermediary between the highest spiritual centre, Shamballa, and the Hierarchy. The Buddha is the Expression of the Wisdom of God, the Embodiment of Light, and the Indicator of the divine Purpose. This will be fixed annually in relation to the Full Moon of May, as is at present the case. It is the great Eastern festival.

3. *The Festival of Goodwill*. This will be the festival of the spirit of humanity—aspiring towards God, seeking conformity with the Will of God and dedicated to the expression of right human relation. This will be fixed annually in relation to the Full Moon of June. It will be a day whereon the spiritual and divine nature of mankind will be recognized. On this festival, for two thousand years, the Christ has represented humanity and has stood before the Hierarchy and in the sight of Shamballa as the God-Man, the Leader of His people and "the Eldest in a great family of brothers" (Romans VIII:29). Each year at that time He has preached the last sermon of the Buddha before the assembled Hierarchy. This will therefore be a festival of deep invocation and appeal, of a basic aspiration towards fellowship, of human and spiritual unity, and will represent the effect in the human consciousness of the work of the Buddha and of the Christ.

These three festivals are already being kept throughout the world, though they are not as yet related to each other, and as part of the unified spiritual Approach of humanity. The time is coming when all three festivals will be kept *simultaneously* throughout the world, and by their means a great spiritual unity will be achieved and the effects of the great Approach so close to us at this time will be stabilized by the united invocation of humanity throughout the planet.

The remaining full moons will constitute lesser festivals, but will be recognized to be also of vital importance. They will establish the divine attributes in the consciousness of man, just as the major festivals establish the three divine aspects. These aspects and qualities will be arrived at and determined by a close study of the nature of a particular constellation or constellations influencing those months. For instance, Capricorn (December) will call attention to the first initiation, the birth of the Christ in the cave of the heart, and indicate the training needed to bring about that great spiritual event in the life of the individual man. I give this one instance to you in order to indicate the possibilities for spiritual unfoldment that could be given through an understanding of these influences, and in order to revivify the ancient faiths by expanding them into their larger undying relationships.

We have, therefore, the following:

Shamballa ....*the Will aspect of God* ....*Wesak*.....................*May Full Moon* (Taurus)

Hierarchy.........*the Love aspect of God* ....*Easter*...................*April Full Moon* (Aries)

Humanity ....*divine Intelligence* ....*Goodwill*.................*June Full Moon* (Gemini)

The remaining nine Full Moons will be concerned with the divine characteristics and their development in mankind.

The Science Of Meditation

In order to partake of these transmissions of energy one should learn to meditate either alone or in a group. In so doing one can employ many techniques. One of these is reflective meditation in which one contemplates a thought; another is receptive meditation in which we open ourselves inwardly and are in a state of receptiveness; and then comes creative meditation where we create thought forms for a particular purpose. In the Zodiac meditations we work with all three stages in a definite order.

We always begin by co-ordinating the threefold personality (body, feeling, thought) in order to become inwardly calm and to be aligned to cosmic events. In so doing we continuously try to dive deeper into our innermost Being until we achieve an awakening to life, a conscious experiencing of our actual Self. Only then can we pass beyond our personal limits entering into a superior cosmic space and establishing contact with the dynamic inflow of energy from the individual signs of the Zodiac.

When we relax and turn within ourselves in meditation, we penetrate the human realm which is called the "Unconscious" in which the archetypal symbols dwell as well as the images of the signs of the Zodiac. Here all religious metaphors, reflections on God and processes of becoming arise. Here too the consciousness awakens to new dimensions which allow one to penetrate the deeper meaning of the qualities of the signs.

We can consciously unlock these energies as they pour in and build a channel to substances on the level of thought, feeling and ether providing direct access to the spiritual meaning of the qualities of the signs. The aspirative forces of each individual are particularly strengthened in group formations; the channel becomes broader, more open, so that one can come into contact with these much more easily. One can of course meditate alone on the signs of the Zodiac in a quiet room.

Once such a 'channel' or 'shaft of light' has been built, it is relatively easy at each Full Moon to come into contact over and over again with different energies. In meditation one can reach such a climax of concentration and identification that specific energies can be transformed under it. The group forms a symbolic reservoir, a vessel or cup into which the individual qualities of the signs flow and are passed on further to humanity. This symbolic presentation, which is suitable for the respective qualities of each sign, represents an important part of the creative phase of meditation.

In this creative process we must remember that a stream of energy only remains in motion when it is passed on through the group to the surrounding world, to our fellow men, to humanity.

It is the law of invocation and evocation which is at work here. The united power of thought, spiritual endeavor and communal invocation of spiritual principles first set the energies in motion. Invocation nearly always calls down an answer, a flowing down of energy or an evocation. It would be misplaced to attempt to claim these energies and qualities for ourselves. This would only cause the stream to become dammed up and to fall victim to the laws of obstinancy, rigidity, crystallization and decay which always carry disruption with them. For this reason the group always turns at the end of each meditation to the whole of Mankind, to which it pours out the energies which it has received.

So in reality the Zodiac meditation is a spiritual service, a process of transformation which one can take part in every month. It is very probable that in primitive times it was in this way that the qualities of the signs of the Zodiac first entered the consciousness of humanity, just as every spiritual impression, every new revelation of divine wisdom originates in this way.

If we belong to a well-functioning meditation group and react particularly intensely to the quality of any one sign—perhaps because our Sun is in it or some other important configuration in our horoscope—then Zodiac meditation is nearly always associated with new realizations. On the basis of certain techniques for the transformation downwards of energies and substances during the period of the Full Moon, and also for the visualization exercise for each of the individual signs, results are nearly always achieved in Zodiac meditations, for "energy follows thoughts".

In the case of meditation through controlled thought—mental meditation—the inner sources and causes of the flow of energy are connected with the manifestation outwardly striven for. The creative process of transforming downwards can be described in the following manner:

The life-force which maintains all manifestation in existence is energy. Man is so equipped that through meditation he can react to energies. A thought clearly orientated during meditation or an image is a means of touching those important aspects of the life-force which we call Light, Love and Life. By interpreting our thoughts correctly we bring them down from the ideal world, direct them towards spiritual activity and in so doing have a transforming effect on life forms. In the Zodiac meditations we should always aspire to this creative process. This goes far beyond many modern forms of meditation; for example "becoming vacant" in which the mind is freed of all its normal functions and a feeling of paralysis rather than that of peace is thus achieved. In this way it is impossible to make full use of the capacity to think in order to interpret inspiration received during meditation.

During the Zodiac meditations an alert and creative participation of the mind is necessary so that we can react to energies and visions as they flow in, registering and interpreting them and storing them in our memory. Very often we experience that inspirations or spiritual impressions are fleeting. If we do not hold on to them with our mind, then we forget them again. Therefore, it is advisable at the end of the meditation—as at the end of dreams—always to write down immediately thoughts and ideas which occurred to us.

A thought or "Seed Thought" of a particular sign of the Zodiac, on which we contemplate "in the light of the Soul", begets new thoughts and mental enlightenment which are interpreted and applied by the practical mind. In other words, in the Zodiac meditations we endeavor to penetrate ever deeper into the qualities of each individual sign, to obtain an ever greater understanding; in this way our attention and joint endeavor is applied to psychic and spiritual relationships.

In order to tune in the group mentally to particular Zodiac qualities, it would be of advantage to read aloud the following texts about each individual sign. The form of meditation to be found at the end of each chapter has been carefully worked out and tested. According to experience the best results can be obtained by using it.

ARIES

Notes • The three great Festivals •
Aries: The sign of new beginnings and of the will •
Prototype of the power of impulse • The symbol of Aries •
The liberating effect of the impulsive power of Aries •
Ego-formation • Self-becoming •
Polarity: Aries-Libra, Axis of encounter •
The ruling planets • The esoteric seed thought of Aries •
The birth of the Self • Creative thinking • Aries-Meditation •

ARIES

ARIES

Notes

Aries	1st sign of the Zodiac
Month	21 March–21 April
Cross	Cardinal
Temperament	Fire
Full Moon	Sun in Aries Moon in Libra
Houses	1st House/7th House Axis of Encounter
Problem Area	Opposition of I and YOU
Planetary Rulers	exoterically Mars esoterically Mercury
Seed Thought	"I come forth and from the plane of mind I rule."

The Three Great Festivals

As in all the realms of nature development in humanity is also subject to the law of ebb and flow. Cyclical periods of spiritual stimulation call forth growth and transformation in human consciousness and give impulse to the course of history.

This cyclical stimulation is of a macro- as well as a microcosmic nature. There are larger and smaller cycles which cut across each other and to which humanity is subject. One of these is the yearly cycle in which the three major festivals of Aries, Taurus and Gemini are to be noted as spiritual climactic points. The first of these is the festival of Easter which is always celebrated in the Aries Month.

With this first Full Moon in the sign Aries a series of quite special Full Moon festivals begins. Aries, Taurus and Gemini represent the prototypes of the three quadruplicities.

In Aries something is always beginning. In nature—the Spring, in the Zodiac—the series of signs, in the aging process—life itself. The festival of Easter too demonstrates a new beginning. The Resurrected Christ is a symbol for this. Here the emphasis lies on the Resurrection and on the new beginning, not so much on the dying and suffering of the Crucifixion. We can all experience the Resurrection in ourselves by joining nature in the blossoming of life in Spring and by turning to new spiritual goals.

Aries: The Sign Of New Beginnings And Of The Will

Aries is the first sign of the Zodiac. It is the sign of the Ego in which Ego-unfoldment begins and a cycle of manifestation is started. It is a Fire sign and transmits the energies of the First Ray or Power of our planetary life. Therefore, Aries represents a principle urging towards unfoldment which emanates from a nucleus or central point or the Ego. From this concentrated nucleus the fiery energy of Will pulsates which can sweep aside with concentrated impetus every obstacle at a stroke.

The sign Aries belongs to the Cardinal Cross, which is esoterically the Cross of the Father of Will and of Omnipotence. Here the Will comes to life, and thus the first step towards incarnation has been taken. Aries "awakens the Will to reach the lowest and there control, to know the uttermost and thus to face all experience"—thus runs an ancient statement.

In accordance with "Esoteric Astrology" by Alice A. Bailey there are three leitmotifs for the sign Aries which all convey the same thought:

1. Express the Will to be and to do.
2. Unfold the power to manifest.

3. Enter into battle for the Lord.
4. Arrive at unity through effort.

In Aries self-becoming has its beginnings, here with the Zodiac the great cycle of struggle towards expression starts. The power of the Ego expresses itself impetuously in Aries, and very often in an unformed manner. Therefore, the Aries individual is impulsive, enterprising and enthusiastic. A power and an energy emanates from him which even shows courage and fearlessness in hopeless situations. Those born under Aries charge forward dragging others with them. They are pioneers who are actively engaged in the progress of the world worrying less about the consequences of their actions. Aries types will always act first and think later. They would like to have success at once and at a stroke, they have little patience for long-term tasks. They need the vitalizing element of the fresh, unique act, and usually they manage everything at the first attempt.

Prototype Of The Power Of Impulse

Aries is so to speak the prototype of the power of impulse which according to Indian philosophy is also called in the Cardinal Cross the Rajah Principle. He therefore has phases when he actively takes part in life full of enthusiasm charging positively at attainable goals; afterwards his energy collapses again and he needs a period of recuperation. He lives according to the law of tension and relaxation, which in the field of psychology can bring about manic-depressive cycles. His psychic curve of Will mounts rapidly, intensely and steeply, only to fall off again after some time, corresponding to the Cardinal Cross or Cross of Impulse in the Zodiac.

The headlong power of the fiery Ram often causes him literally to shoot beyond his goal. It is characteristic of this sign to overshoot and to go too far. He finds it difficult to keep within limits, not only his own but even more those of others. This causes many difficulties in his relations with his fellow human beings. The impulsive Aries often comes into conflict with the qualities of patience, tact, form, moderation and propriety. The ability to measure out and to moderate his powers is an exercise with which the Aries person is usually occupied for his whole life.

On the other hand, it is a spiritual task of Aries to tear away hardened bounderies and to overcome the confines and barriers built through fear so that life may progress and unfold.

The Symbol Of Aries ♈

If we consider the symbol of the sign Aries, we can also see it in people's faces. The eyebrows with the upper ridge of the nose form the Aries symbol. It points to a marked personal self-consciousness with a strong power to succeed, impulsiveness and a penetrating, spiritual ability, but also to the tendency to impetuosity, anger, defensiveness, etc.

As we have seen, Aries is the sign of new beginnings and new developments. We can also see this in nature. We find the Aries symbol in buds and leaves once they have burst open. They embody new life and the beginning of a new cycle. Here as well the outer covering is burst by inner, driving power which breaks all bounds to create space for the new life.

This process of breaking through is induced by the dynamic power of the indwelling Will of our own Ego. It can work destructively as well as creatively, according to how it is applied.

The Liberating Effect Of The Impulsive Power Of Aries

In the Aries month we all have an increased opportunity to work with this dynamic Aries power. At the same time it is a purifying Fire force which enables us to clear away old unwanted circumstances. Just as we can set to work in the Spring with the spring-cleaning, so we can also clean out our personality and free it from unwanted conditions. Above all the dross which has built up during the Winter months can now be put right again in a healthy manner by purifying cures and a sensible diet. We can similarly dissolve and cast off spiritual burdens, anxieties and oppressing worries through the vitalizing element of the Aries energy by leaving the old behind us and by adjusting ourselves with confidence to the new and better.

The Risen Christ says to us "Behold, I make all things new". Here the vitalizing Aries-element appears as a spring of water within us; it is the Christ-force, the universal force of Love which opens new springs of life. We want to open ourselves to it in a very special way in the Aries month. Once the force of love is flowing freely through us, we can also experience ourselves anew as Ego, as personality and learn to love anew.

Ego-formation

Ego-unfoldment begins in Aries; the Ram needs a strong Ego-center for his path of development, that is, a stable self-certainty. If we still have not fully developed our Ego, we can now work on our Ego-formation by freeing ourselves, for example, from too great a dependence on our environment, by recognizing ourselves and by accepting ourselves as we are.

For if we wish to succeed in the world and in life, we need a form appropriate to the world, we need a resistant Ego. If this fails, all our external influences can flow on through us and we become the plaything of our surroundings. If on the other hand our Ego is too strongly defined, then there is a danger that this Ego will become hardened; the form has become closed—nothing can flow in and nothing can flow out. Such a person is the captive of his Ego-form, as if he were a captive in prison; he is neither accessible to his fellow men nor permeable to his own inner Being. In the Aries month we can apply the impulsive power to tear down the walls which we have erected around us in false self-defense.

The Aries type is in general a person with a definite Ego-consciousness. Aries is indeed the first sign of the Cardinal Cross, and it is completely in order that the person with an emphasized Aries will be driven on by internal and external energies to activity for the purpose of creating a new and better world. Yet the danger always exists for him that he will attempt with Ego-emphasized ambition to outdo others, whether it is in knowledge, know-how, in education or in his profession. An immoderate estimation of one's personal significance and an unwholesome spirit of competitiveness easily arise from these power struggles. The strong tendency of this type to extraversion all too often causes him to fight out problems and conflicts in battle with the external world and less within his own Self. The success which he attains in the world he usually ascribes to his own powers and builds his self-consciousness upon them.

In the case of spiritually orientated people however, it is in reality above all a matter of new birth, of the birth of the true Self, which partakes of eternal existence. We should especially open and prepare ourselves for this new birth in the Aries month.

It is always a help in all situations when we return to the starting point. Here we can undertake corrections, put right mistakes and begin again. At the starting point we also find our inner "Self". Here we shall find all the assistance we need, it comes from our deepest source of life which leads as an energy emitting force and as "I AM" to "I WILL" and "I CAN". We also recognize that we are being used, that it is up to us. With such thoughts our powers grow and we are able to clear away unpleasant circumstances and to create once again order within ourselves and in our surroundings so that the new life can prosper which has its beginning in Aries.

Self-Becoming

The problem of self-becoming is one of the fundamental themes of human existence. In a spiritual sense self-becoming also depends on the acquirement of the correct Ego-consciousness, that is, the establishment of the true center. It is a fact that an individual needs an Ego-center so that spiritual energies can flow into a usable vessel. Whoever does not possess one, must build one up; whoever has too much of one, must become permeable.

In the first instance it is a matter of simply becoming conscious of one's own Ego. Many spiritually striving people ask themselves whether they do not feed their egoism when they concentrate on their Ego. The exact opposite is the case. If we do not know our Ego and lead an insufficiently conscious life, then it rules us and does with us and our surroundings what it will. If we wish to control our Ego-powers, we must know our Ego exactly and become familiar with the potentialities and effects of its powers in operation. An overweak Ego is just as much an obstacle in life as a hardened one. Therefore, we must first strive for a secure Ego-consciousness before we can handle spiritual energies without risk. Our relationship to our environment, to ourselves, to our innermost Being and to the transcendental depends on this.

With regard to Ego-becoming we must say "yes" to ourselves, stepping forward and showing ourselves to the world in the certainty "I am thus, I think thus and act thus. I am not governed by the opinions of others, but I am what I am."

Most people are afraid of presenting themselves as they really are. They are afraid of being falsely judged or of showing their weaknesses to others.

The newly born Being, the Self, which is manifested for the first time in Aries is still unformed, insecure and easily hurt and is threatened by unknown forces. It requires succour and help from without and from within. If the world has a too intensive effect on this infant Being, it builds a defensive mechanism for its own protection. This is quite natural in childhood, but one easily loses one's identity if this is carried over into adulthood. For whoever is too occupied with protecting himself against the external world and who at the same time wishes to master all demands from without cannot get round to learning about his own nature, to developing and securing it and to establishing the relationship to the external world suitable to his inner Self.

It becomes disastrous when we never stop being constrained and defined by the behaviour patterns formed in childhood. Indeed, in the years of early development so-called "virtuous apparent Ego-forms" are built up which often have little to do with the innermost being. At a certain point in development one must free oneself from these forms of defense and from the all too idealistic picture of one's own person so that one may in all honesty and reality become oneself. Defense mechanisms and apparent Ego-forms may have been of great value at a particular time, yet as an adult one should give up both so that the true Self can break through and fulfill itself. That is a difficult but necessary process.

For a long time we believe that we must defend our own Imago, our ideal picture of ourselves. We believe that masks or role functions might protect us from exposure. But this is a delusion for in the end we feel alienated from ourselves because we have continuously distanced ourselves from ourselves. Then we live in the constant fear of being recognized by others. Behind a thousand masks we hide our insecurity, our confusion and our loneliness. The simple thought that others could recognize our weaknesses seizes us with anxiety and we shut ourselves off. In desperation we are continuously finding new facades behind which we can hide and which protect us from knowing, comprehending looks.

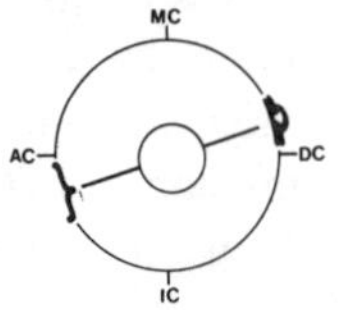

Polarity: Aries-Libra
Axis of Encounter

The signs Aries and Libra correspond to the First and Seventh houses which represent the Axis of Encounter (q.v. "Man and His World"). Just such a comprehending look from a YOU would be our salvation and a great help during self-becoming. We know this deep within ourselves. If we are honest with ourselves, we are longing to be recognized by others for what we really are. But this recognition must be bound up with being accepted—with love. That is the only thing which gives us security. Once we have experienced that we have a value and that we mean something to someone, then we are free. But we do not show this need to be accepted. Or do not mention it, we do not dare to do either, we are afraid that deep within ourselves we have no value and that others may see this and reject us. Thus, we are all playing a desperate game of hide-and-seek: a secure facade without and a shaking child within. However, this attitude hinders us from becoming genuine human beings. Self-knowledge is only possible if we expose ourself to it by experiencing ourselves in the encounter with others, honestly and openly. When we open ourselves spontaneously to other people, and in so doing to love, through which all opportunities of transformation come and which tears down all barriers, then the opposite sign to Aries—Libra—will certainly become activated: the encounter between EGO and YOU becomes possible. Aries people should therefore always be prepared to encounter the YOU openly and honestly and to show themselves as they really are. Only in the encounter with others—in a group or in a love affair—can that Self be offered which is waiting within for recognition and acceptance.

The Ruling Planets ♂ ☿

As is well-known Aries is ruled by Mars, the esoteric Ruler being Mercury. With the help of Mercury proper human relationships can be established. It is a planet of the mind and of intelligent communication whose task it is to think first and then to act, not like Mars which "shoots first and asks questions later" and which often offends other people by its uncooth manner without even noticing it.

In the case of someone with the Sun in Aries, the warlike Martian qualities will predominate, but if he develops spiritually, the moderating influence of Mercury will gradually become stronger. In this way the intelligence becomes powerful. In Aries, as in no other sign, it is pronounced how everything is initiated, caused or hindered by itself, for everything that he thinks pushes towards manifestation and realization. Only he can break up in turn thought forms of fear, depression or discouragement with the same creative force with which he erected them. Thus the Aries dominated individual is subject to a constant toing and froing, to the erection and destruction of forms and manic-depressive fluctuations of feeling which are very difficult to control.

Cleansing and purifying are also concerned here: with Mars through fire, war and combat and with Mercury through spiritual vision, that is, the capacity to recognize and to differentiate. In this way the combat is raised to the mental level and higher processes of thought. With the help of will-power and the capacity to differentiate, all negative and undesired thoughts and apparent Ego-forms may be rejected and eliminated and only those thoughts allowed which are necessary for the realization of the true Self.

Mercury becomes the enlightening principle which frees the mind. It leads people through life and enables them to use their combative powers for the carrying through of creative ideas which are not only of value to their individual Egos but also to as large a number of people as possible.

The Esoteric Seed Thought Of Aries Runs

I come forth and from the plane of mind I rule.

In esoteric writings Aries is called the "birth place of divine thoughts." It is not only souls which urge towards incarnation in Aries, and which are ruled by Mars until such time as they have attained reorientation and have become receptive to the influence of Mercury, but also divine thoughts, new ideas which wish to be born into our minds and to become leading life motifs. We should be receptive to these today in the meditation.

Let Us Summarize:

Aries is the sign of beginnings, of birth, of ideas which are formed in the mind enveloping themselves in substance so that they may be born. Thus, we must inwardly pay careful attention to that which wants to be manifested through us; whether it is our inner Self or whether it is a new idea which occurs to us and which we are to express; an idea, an enthusiastic spark which for one tiny moment awakens within us and which can change our whole life at a stroke. From this moment we are no longer the same person, something new has been born into us. In a higher sense it is the birth of Christ in the heart, the birth of the true Self in us, which can be carried out through the power of Aries and with the help of the higher Will.

The Birth Of The Self

At every birth the powers of thrusting, of bursting outer coverings are necessary. Just as the chicken breaks the shell of the egg to reach the light of day, so the inner Self at self-becoming or rebirth breaks the outer coverings; apparent Ego-forms, masks and hardened barriers fall away. Then we indeed stand there uncovered and must find our way. In a certain sense we must always cross a frontier when we wish to penetrate into a higher dimension of Being. We push into new regions where we still do not know our way. Therefore, we should be warily quiet so that we can pay attention to our intuitive direction. If we push forwards rashly and believe we can "conquer heaven at a stroke" with the dynamic, combative power of Aries, then we shall suffer setbacks. Therefore, orientation and careful information about the new regions is necessary. Mercury, as the esoteric Ruler, serves us as a source of information and arbiter.

Creative Thinking

Through creative thinking we can support the process of rebirth. We can work creatively on the mental plane when we have recognized and tested our power of thinking. Through thinking alone can we desire the good, the best and that which promotes development for ourselves and for all humanity and in this way co-operate in the improvement of human affairs.

Thinking is powerful in Aries, yet the connection between concrete and abstract thinking should be striven for in order to escape from the usual "thinking in circles". Higher thought is the instrument of intuition with which we may break through the shell of our present knowledge and penetrate into regions which lie outside our capacity of comprehension, where completely new and never before existing ideas can be recognized, however, and accommodated within concrete thinking.

As a group we take part in this creative process during every meditation, for here we endeavor in particular to bring new ideas about the special Zodiac qualities into our consciousness and to pass them on to humanity. We thus serve higher ideas as a connecting channel on the mental plane, as a tool, through which Light and Love can then flow into the hearts of Men. Today we dedicate ourselves anew, our little Egos and our group to the service of the world.

Thus we begin the meditation.

Aries Meditation

1. Stage: Preparation

During the meditation we sit with a straight back. We close our eyes, but may open them occasionally if tensions arise. We rest our hands on our thighs and place our feet together. We achieve the greatest relaxation of the body by transferring our inner focus to the middle of our body. We let the upper part of our body turn slightly in a circular motion until we have the sensation of sitting at the focal point, at the Hara.

The breath also has a part to play in the preparation for the meditation. We breathe in and out four times. On exhaling we say "Let go—Relax", then we hold our breath and think "Become one", on inhaling "Become new", we hold our breath, "Be yourself". We do this a few times.

2. Stage: Alignment

Alignment of the threefold personality, physical, emotional and mental with the Soul. For this exercise in integration we use after every stage the Sacred Word OM in order to shut out all disruptive vibrations.

The Physical Body

Our physical body rests calmly and quietly on the chair, we are borne by the chair, secure in the house. OM

The Emotional Body

We calm our emotions by imagining a sheet of blue water in which the Sun or the Moon is reflected. OM

The Mental Body

Thoughts come and go. I remain quite calm listening in to myself, looking at my thoughts, I do not let myself be distracted. OM

Alignment With The Soul

We are inwardly secure, attuned to the good and the beautiful, quite prepared to come into contact with our innermost Being.

We collect our attention together at that place in the head which we exercise when thinking, the brain. Then we feel into our forehead letting our muscles become quite relaxed there. The forehead becomes smooth, the face appears friendly and calm.

Now we let the focal point of our consciousness glide slowly down from within our head—as a snail crawls—between the jaws, through the neck, into the upper breast, further down, to the middle, behind the breastbone, to the level of the heart. Now we are at the place to which we point when we say "I". We point our finger at ourselves and think "I". We attempt to perceive an agitation of the Ego and to detect the way in which we experience this, in which it reacts within us.

3. Stage: Ego-Meditation

"I am. I find myself here—now; in this room, at this time, on this chair. In real fact, undeniably, I am here, I am. I simply find myself to be. I can see, touch, perceive myself. I am here. I am absolutely here. I cannot shake the fact. I AM. I cannot leave my skin. I cannot simply climb out and say, now it's over. This absoluteness is strong and unalterable. As if I had been planted: there you are, and now you are there. Where does this force, this power come from which creates such constancy of my Being, to the end that I am always here?"

"I want to experience my Ego as it really is. Everything that is foreign to my Being, which does not belong to me, I reject, sending it back with my will-power to the periphery of my consciousness. My power of resistance grows and defends itself against the false thoughts of anxiety, discouragement and self-depreciation. I am strong in my own center."

4. Stage: Aries Visualization Exercise

I imagine within me a point of light, slowly it becomes larger and larger and spreads over my whole body brightening the dark space around me. I see a door before me. I approach it knowing that I must go out that way in order to escape the restriction of the Ego. I open the door, bright daylight streams in. I step out to see a broad horizon, presenting myself to the world as I am. Free from fear and doubt I open myself completely letting the Light and Love which is in me and the world stream through me. I inhale deeply and meditate on the Seed Thought:

I come forth and from the plane of mind I rule.

5. Stage: Group Endeavor

We extend our consciousness out over our surroundings and join with the people around us and with all those who approach the spiritual energies at Full Moon in meditation. We form a group unity on the mental plane receptive to the cosmic energies which are now available. We behold a path of light stretching from humanity to that source where the Love of God dwells, which is expressed on our planet through Christ. We feel ourselves to be enclosed within this Love and dedicate the group to the service of the world.

We imagine how we all raise together a cup into the air in highly concentrated inner aspiration, in an appeal to the spiritual powers of light and love which flow into our receptive consciousness and symbolically into the raised cup.

We raise our hands very slowly.

> "By forgetting the things which lie behind us we turn resolutely to our new spiritual opportunities.
>
> We dedicate ourselves anew to the service of the coming time and desire to do everything to prepare the hearts and the minds of humanity for it."

6. Stage: Transmission To Humanity

We slowly lower our hands and turn to humanity. We let this living stream of the energy of Light, Love and creative Will flow through us into the consciousness of Mankind and to spread itself.

In so doing we imagine how these powers radiate from numberless points of light, from a net of light spread out over our planet reaching all those in whose hands the fate of humanity lies. Then together we transmit the energy stream to humanity through the Great Invocation.

THE GREAT INVOCATION

From the point of Light within the Mind of God
Let light stream forth into the minds of men.
Let Light descend on Earth.

From the point of Love within the Heart of God
Let love stream forth into the hearts of men.
May Christ return to Earth.

From the centre where the Will of God is known
Let purpose guide the little wills of men—
The purpose which the Masters know and serve.

From the centre which we call the race of men
Let the Plan of Love and Light work out
And may it seal the door where evil dwells.

Let Light and Love and Power restore the Plan on Earth.

Completion Of The Meditation

We open our eyes inhaling and exhaling once deeply. We move our head, our neck, our shoulders, our feet, our hands. Then we extend to each other our hands, look into each other's eyes and bow before each other.

TAURUS

Notes • The Wesak-Festival • The four noble truths of Buddha • Transmission of Energies • Taurus qualities • The Taurus Symbol • The developed Taurus Type • The spiritual task • Two directions of development • Self-Acceptance Confidence in life, thankfulness and harmlessness • The planetary rulers • The spiritual crisis of Taurus • Polarity: Taurus-Scorpio. Axis of Possession • Enlightenment • The esoteric seed thought of Taurus • The process of transmission. the Wesak Festival • Taurus-Meditation •

TAURUS

TAURUS

Notes

Taurus	2nd sign of the Zodiac
Month	22 April–21 May
Cross	Fixed
Temperament	Earth
Full Moon	Sun in Taurus Moon in Scorpio
Houses	2nd House/8th House Axis of Possession
Problem Area	One's own possessions— other's possessions
Planetary Rulers	exoterically Venus esoterically Vulcan
Seed Thought	"I see, and when the Eye is opened, all is illumined."

With the last Full Moon in Aries a series of Full Moon Festivals began which correspond to the first quadrant of the Zodiac. The first three signs represent the prototypes of the three Crosses: Aries the Cardinal Cross, Taurus the Fixed Cross and Gemini the Mutable Cross.

As a further reminder:

In Aries an impulse, an idea is conceived, created, initiated. It arises in the mind and is stored away in the desire body. Here the idea is taken up by desire, aspiration or the Will, processed and brought to realization. This demands an inner adjustment to work which must be done, an acceptance of recognized tasks and opportunities, a conquering of indolence and egoistic desires as well as the willingness to accept sacrifices in order to realize the envisaged idea.

The Wesak Festival

As has already been mentioned the Taurus Festival is one of the most important in the year. It is associated with Buddha who was born under Taurus. In the Buddhist religion it is at the Wesak Festival that many people make a pilgrimage to a certain place to receive the blessing of the Buddha there. According to an old tradition the Divine Idea is handed over symbolically by the Guardians of the Plan in a small valley in the Himalayas to Christ and his assembled disciples. This is supposed to have been happening annually on the spiritual plane for thousands of years and means for the Buddha that he must leave his elevated place to make a spiritual sacrifice so that new energies may be passed on to humanity for its further development.

For a better understanding of our special meditation work at today's Full Moon it is a good idea if we have a closer knowledge of this process of transmission or of the transformation downwards of spiritual energies and if we imagine to ourselves this ceremony of transference during the meditation. I shall give you a short description of the ceremony which is a symbolic representation of the process of transmission:

Buddha appears as a small point of light in heaven becoming ever larger as he approaches the Earth. In a small bottle-shaped valley in the Himalayas the assembled disciples are waiting in deep contemplation. Christ is standing at the highest point looking towards the Buddha in preparation to receive the transfer of energy. He gives Christ his blessing and passes the enlightened message to him. Then he disappears slowly. The energies flow through Christ to humanity. This transmission to humanity is celebrated in June at the Gemini Full Moon.

The Four Noble Truths Of Buddha

The teaching of the Buddha is strongly connected with the sign Taurus. In his Four Noble Truths he explained the cause of human difficulties and pointed to the means by which these can be solved. His message can be summarized in simple words—it corresponds to the spiritual task of Taurus: "Cease to identify yourselves with material things; gain a proper sense of spiritual values; cease regarding possessions and earthly existence as of major importance; follow the Noble Eightfold Path which is the path of right relations—right relations to God and to each other—and thus be happy."

This ancient message is as new today as it was when Buddha spoke these words on earth. It was on the foundation of his teaching that Christ was able to establish Love on Earth. It then became possible for Men to tread the enlightened way which leads back to the divine source of Light and Love.

Transmission Of Energies

Buddha, whose Festival is always held at the May Full Moon, acts today as the agent of that "Great Life" in whom we live and move and have our Being. Year after year ever since Buddha achieved his goal of illumination, an effort has been made to increase the flow of the true Light into the world and to direct it as wisdom, experience and understanding into the minds of Men. At each Full Moon in May this has been the effort of the spiritual forces of our planet. Today we can participate consciously in receiving these energies or qualities of the Light and in passing them on to humanity. We wish to make an effort to serve in a comprehensible manner as the transmitter of spiritual energies which on this day flow into humanity, and we must try to perceive the Divine Will or Plan for the immediate future.

This knowledge justifies our endeavor to come together here and to meditate communally. The Zodiac meditation is—thus considered—in reality a service and serves to a lesser extent personal purposes.

Qualities of wisdom, intelligence and of right conduct are transmitted. Indeed, these are always present on Earth, but they are particularly strong at the May Full Moon so that we can not only receive new understanding of our own life but can also pray for more light and understanding for those who are responsible for the fate of Mankind. The forces of enlightenment always work through those who truly love their fellowmen and who wish to assist them spiritually.

Taurus Qualities

You may well justifiably ask why Taurus in particular should be associated with the great process of transmission of the Wesak Festival. Normally one considers the Taurus individual to be more concerned with the material values of our existence. Let us examine the qualities of the sign Taurus more closely and explore the connections.

The sign Taurus belongs to the Fixed Cross and it is an Earth sign. Those born under Taurus therefore have a steady Will, constancy and durability and a strong desire nature. This can be directed to both material as well as spiritual things. The desire or feeling nature of a person is the lowest aspect of the spiritual Will and has a dominant effect when it is directed towards a definite goal. Taurus individuals can only decide on something with difficulty, but once they have decided and their ambition and interest have been awakened, then they will only let go with difficulty. Whatever they want with their concentrated will-power they can attain relatively easily. The desire body has, through the influence of Taurus, the special ability of "self-appropriation".

The Taurus Symbol ♉

This is also represented through the symbolic drawing of the Bull. The bowl signifies the acceptance of things coming from without, whether they be material or spiritual, good or bad. The massively enclosed circle demonstrates that what is accepted is preserved firmly enclosed in the kernel. When this appropriation concerns the material, then money, possessions and property are acquired. In the area of the spirit or of the ideal, spiritual values, genuine substance, ideals, currents of other spheres or even illumination are perceived and processed.

The enclosed circle of the Taurus symbol also represents those creative powers which slumber hidden only waiting to come to light. That can occur in the greatest excitement when the Bull loses his patience or, on the other hand, in the highest spiritual aspiration. Then the contents, the captured and stored power, pours out into the consciousness. Often a ray of recognition breaks through illuminating the situation at a stroke and bringing the necessary understanding. Then the Taurus individual can free himself in a flash from his chains throwing himself onto a new path. As soon as the recognition lights up, he charges forward; mighty powers are unleashed and he frees himself irrevocably from people and things who have become a hinderance to him.

Taureans are the true possessors of spiritual and material values. They are as acquainted with possessions as with their own bodies. They grow so to speak out of their own potency into the imagined world so that it is awakened to life by their own power and energy, although it may also become at the same time a thousandfold chain. This occurs because not only the observed surface but also the substance with all its nerves lying beneath becomes bodily felt and perceived. This is also the key to the rare gift of actualization, for the tangibly perceived world does not let the Taurean go until it has become reality.

The Developed Taurus Type

In the developed Taurus type the power of desire is transformed into spiritual striving, his aim is the higher values of existence. This inner process of transformation requires detachment from chains and bonds which have arisen during the period of establishment, as well as a renunciation of the satisfaction of egoistic and material desires. This is a difficult process and demands the enlightenment of the mind as well as the awakening of the desire for good, not only for oneself but also for the largest possible number of people. This takes place through the mobilization of the forces of the opposite sign Scorpio whose psychological and spiritual power of transformation through eternal "death and becoming" irradiate Taurus.

Here begins the treading of the spiritual path at whose edge the chains and bonds which we have overcome are left behind like dead forms. However, this can only be accomplished through the higher function of the spiritual Will. This spiritual Will can become powerful in Taurus and operate as a sacrificial Will. Once a spiritual idea has been perceived, then a person born under Taurus will do everything to realize this idea in daily life. No sacrifice, no effort is too great for him when he is serving spiritual aims. The accomplishment of an achievement and the realization of an ideal are always associated with a sacrifice where the smaller is offered for the greater. This is a characteristic aspect of the laws of evolution and the leading thought of the whole process of creation.

This spirit of sacrifice always appears when we have attained the Will of God or the Shamballa force itself to a modest extent. Today at the Taurus Full Moon this energy is conveyed directly to humanity and should awaken the desire in us to partake consciously of this Will and its divine spirit of sacrifice.

The Spiritual Task

The spiritual task of the sign Taurus in particular is giving, the dedication of oneself to something higher, the joyful renunciation of personal interests in favor of the whole or for the benefit of a thing, a group or of an ideal. During these days of Full Moon and during the whole Taurus month we can grow beyond ourselves; reform our accustomed life in order to dedicate ourselves more extensively to spiritual goals and to bring our life into harmony with the laws of evolution or with the divine plan as it is expressed esoterically.

That is to say, we should be prepared to make some sort of sacrifice, to renounce something which we should like to have for ourselves so that we may rank among the multitude of those who have always utilized their powers in the service of others. Then a vitalizing joy awakens within us which arises from the experience of unity with others, and thus from spiritual sources, and can always be sensed when we have won a victory over ourselves.

Two Directions Of Development

In the sign Taurus, as in all other signs, there are two directions of development. One is directed upwards, the other downwards.

In the average man, as in the mass, the power of desire becomes craving, as an inner urge to make everything even better and more pleasant. How often one observes that craving goes beyond what is attainable. We want to have everything better than others. From this feeling envy develops which is always making comparisons with others and which is satisfied with nothing. In order to curb craving and aspirative force and to bring the desire nature under control, it is important to cultivate thankfulness and satisfaction. We should once again turn our eyes to what is available around us and to recognize the beautiful and the wonderful of the present.

Here the esoteric Seed Thought of Taurus becomes important:

I see, and when the eye is opened, all is illumined.

Then everything is beautiful, good and pleasing. The power of desire reverts within itself and is capable of recognizing the good and the beautiful and to see it in all things, in relation to myself and to my fellow men, in relation to what has befallen me and to what I made of it. Thankfulness and the glorification of the good and the beautiful are positive qualities of the desire nature. I can cultivate them within me during the Taurus month and adapt myself to them with particular intensity. I can wish the good, expect the beautiful and recognize the past as meaningful. Even if it was unpleasant, or indeed terrible things that I experienced, that fell to my lot or were done to me, I can still adapt myself consciously to them and see the deeper meaning in everything. If I am honest, everything that happened to me had a meaning, brought me understanding and led me a little further on my way.

Self-Acceptance

This illuminating and saving force has an effect in the present in that I accept what is allotted to me. Taking, accepting and possessing are typical Taurus attributes. In my own development I must be prepared to accept myself and my fate. I must not resist, stubbornly and sulkily. I must learn to accept what is reality and look with fully conscious and open eyes at my immediate environment and at myself, recognizing clearly and realistically what I am and what I have to give the world. This recognition of one's own value is important today because one's own capacity to accept the responsibility of doing something for the improvement of the conditions in the world grows simultaneously from it. To say yes to ourselves and to everything is to take possession of our own world. We gain ground, expand and spread ourselves out. In this act of acceptance a redeeming and saving force lies hidden. It demolishes the walls which I have erected in false self-defense between myself and my fellow men, between myself and the divine powers. Each refusal to accept reality brings me into difficulties. I erect barriers and hide behind my own demands becoming impermeable to the new and the beautiful which wants to grow and prosper within me and in nature. I must not refuse to feed the inner life, clinging fast with anxiety to existing things, to apparent material security. If I do that and hold fast covetously to my possessions or to my achievements, I detach myself from the life forces.

It is therefore beneficial to examine today whether we have erected such walls around us and to begin to dismantle them. The best way of doing this is self-acceptance, where we show ourselves to be satisfied with and thankful for the life which pulsates within us. If we have thankfulness in our hearts, then we can also experience love again which brings us happiness and joy. Our heart center opens and we become receptive to the inner Being within us. If we are too busy with other unimportant things, then we often do not notice this at all and let opportunities pass us by. Therefore, we must remain still today, being alert and attuned utterly and completely to the present waiting in quiet certainty for that which wishes to become here.

Just as in the Aries month the buds in nature burst open through the impulse giving, penetrating power of the Cardinal Cross, so now in the Taurus month of May the blossom wants to grow forth—those buds which were hidden within but present all the time in Winter. In order to become aware of our Soul, which, like the bud, wants to reach unfoldment within us, we must look inwards, becoming inwardly quite still and opening ourselves to what has been slumbering within us for a long time and what is waiting to come to the light of day. That could be for example hidden talents. Therefore, the neck is important in Taurus, for we must bow our head learning to look into ourselves and to be able to stay quiet and thankful.

Confidence In Life, Thankfulness And Harmlessness

The joyful expectation of good also brings forth the Taurus confidence in life, confidence in the life-sustaining forces of nature, the security that one will always have everything that is necessary for life. In reality we need far less than we imagine. The proverbial benevolence of the Taurean is also based on this confidence in nature and God. This is also a part of that power of thankfulness, innocence and naivity which only expects the good and the beautiful and which awakens as from the sleep of Sleeping Beauty when disillusion arrives and reality makes itself felt in the form of painful experience. This is so incomprehensible for a Taurean that he may be deprived of his composure and thrown off his path. Taurus however always needs repeatedly such shaking experiences so that fixed and hardened states of consciousness may be broken up and development may remain in motion. Benevolence and blindness then become genuine harmlessness in the enlightened Taurean.

Harmlessness is not naive credulity, which is passive and unintelligent, but an active attunement to life born of a genuine practical wisdom. Genuine harmlessness is charged with psychic and spiritual energies and borne by the recognition and esteem of the Divine in all things and by the knowledge of the good and the beautiful in creation. This knowledge of the beautiful, this maintenance of faith, vision, the Good and the Light is the spiritual force of the enlightened Buddha and a special task of those born under Taurus. Taurus has the ability through its purposeful Will to carry forward the vision or the Light like a dynamic goal. He always knows what is to be done next. Nothing can distract him from going the right way, even if this way is burdensome. If he has a goal, he is ready to exert himself. Calmly he takes on burdens, his own and those of others. He renounces the satisfaction of his own desires. No sacrifice is too great for him. Patiently he advances step by step towards his goal to which he has dedicated himself with his whole heart.

The Planetary Rulers ♀ ¥

We recognize Venus as the Ruler of Taurus with her strong desire for beauty, comfort and security. Taurus cannot take losses lightly, neither material and financial nor spiritual and substantial. He immediately tries to counteract every endangering of his inner peace and comfort and thus to secure them. He does everything in his power to avoid losses or to compensate for them immediately so that the state of security and harmony which he has achieved may be maintained. That is a typical influence of Venus.

The esoteric Ruler of Taurus is Vulcan, a planet which up to now has not been recognized in traditional astrology. It is supposed to be situated between Mercury and the Sun and corresponds to the First Ray. Therefore, its effect is connected with Will and power.

The Spiritual Crisis Of Taurus

This mighty power which flows through the raging Bull must of course first be refined before it can operate prosperously. As we have seen he must transform the longing of his desire nature into spiritual endeavor and sacrificial Will and then use his powers for the realization of the Divine Will. To this purpose a particular reversal or change is necessary. This inner crisis of the Taurean on the spiritual path is identical to the experience of Christ in the Garden of Gethsemane when he had to renounce his own Will to complete the Divine Will. "Not my will, but Thine, be done." This is called in esoteric-psychological literature the "Gethsemane Experience" in which the individual must experience the depths of being alone as he stands completely isolated. He is detached from that which is above and from that which is below. It is a highly dramatic moment when all longing is renounced and the Will of God or the Plan is recognized and accepted as the only goal worth striving for. Therefore, the spiritually orientated Taurean is always being put to the test to see whether he is strong enough to tread further on the way of service. Such experiences are often felt during the Taurus month.

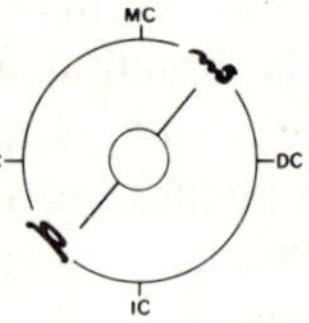

Polarity: Taurus-Scorpio
Axis Of Possession

In the sign Taurus the destructive side of Vulcan and thus of the First Ray must be conquered. Then the Taurean can function as the "Former of Souls"—his own included. He must strive for a clear vision, a pure, joyful Will, for the building of a better world and the extinguishing of personal longing. During this process of formation great changes in consciousness occur and fundamental changes are brought about by this sign—in association with its polar opposite Scorpio, one of the most difficult signs in the Zodiac. Under the assault of this energy of change profound ruptions and transformations of character occur in quality and direction. Taurus is a dangerous sign because its destructive aspects can easily be overemphasized and applied intelligently to any situation. It is important for Taureans to realize that they must make their energies, amassed in this and in previous lives, available for spiritual goals. Taureans are souls who must be "born again in spirit". It is their task to complete the great work of transmutation from a lower to a higher octave of consciousness.

The powers of desire or Will which are at work in Taurus are described thus in "Esoteric Astrology" by Alice A. Bailey: "Taurus forges the instruments of constructive living or of destruction; it forges the chains which bind or creates the key which unlocks the mystery of life; it is this forging process, with its constant clamour, which is going on at this time in a most potent manner. Vulcan controls the anvil-like processes of time and strikes the blow which shapes the metal into that which is desired, and this is true today as never before. He is who is forging the way for the coming Avatar."

Enlightenment

There are two key words for Taurus—the power of desire on the material plane and illumination or enlightenment on the spiritual. Enlightenment comes at the advanced stage when the small personal Will has become one with the Divine Will. Taurus then has the enlightened "one eye" which unswervingly looks at the Light of the final goal, which corresponds to contemplation or the continuity of consciousness. The Buddha, as a person born under Taurus, is an example of this.

The Esoteric Seed Thought Of Taurus Runs:

I see, and when the Eye is opened, all is illumined.

The person born under Taurus must therefore become seeing. Blindness must give way to spiritual vision, to the correct inner adjustment. This will at last drive out self-produced illusions and delusions as well as the self-pity which afflicts him when he cannot get what he wants.

In the Taurus month we should cultivate our vision, for this will vitalize our activities, purify our feelings and uplift our mind. We attain the insight that the only valuable possession which we can have is a spiritual motivation or goal which preserves us from sinking into materialism. The blindness of longing needs the direction of a spiritually perceived vision.

The mind must be enlightened when it is a question of spiritual matters. The eye should be opened upwards so that one can see what must be done next in the realization of the Plan. One must become blind downwards in the direction of the material side of life; then material needs and anxieties will no longer throw us from our path. This is the readjustment of the lights which takes place as soon as one has become spiritually awakened and seeing.

Once the Taurean has become seeing, he knows exactly what he has to do; the way lies lit and clear before him—darkness, loneliness and desperation come to an end. He becomes receptive to the needs of others and at the same time to his inner direction which gives him correct orientation. He will no longer charge blindly forwards, but will go along the way of liberation full of insight—the way which leads to his own liberation and which will at the same time spur on to those activities which bring about the redemption of others.

Thus he will become a valuable co-worker in the Plan or in ambitious projects for relieving the needs of humanity and for establishing better conditions for all on this Earth.

In ancient texts Taurus is described as "the eye of enlightenment", "the mother of sacrifice", the "interpreter of the Divine Voice", "the enlightened Buddha".

The Process Of Transmission: The Wesak Festival

Before we start the meditation, I should like once again to outline and briefly summarize the process of transmission described at the beginning. A ritual which, year in, year out, is supposed to take place in the Taurus month in a valley in the Himalayas.

As we have seen, enlightenment effects the mental plane through goal-orientated volition, the physical plane through the testimony of wisdom and skillful action and the emotional plane through the motive of loving understanding. It is always these three aspects of human thinking, desiring and action through which the forces of Light can flow. The ceremony of the daily life of our "Planetary Logos" expresses itself through tones and the music of the spheres which break, carried by the waves of color, on the shores of the three worlds of human evolution. "As in the microcosm, thus in the macrocosm", as the saying runs. Looked at in the broader context, it is thus three great Beings who control and receive those energies and who come actively into contact during the five days of the Full Moon. They are these:

1. The Lord of the World, the Light of Life itself.
2. Buddha, the Lord of Wisdom who transmits spiritual light and unveils divine purposes.
3. Christ, the Lord of Love who conveys the pleas of Mankind and acts with authority for the distribution of the forces of enlightenment.

Expressed esoterically, these three aspects of Light find their most perfect expression in the Lord of the World, the "Planetary Logos" and in his reflexion through the Buddha and Christ—one having brought enlightenment to the world and the other having proven the reality of the Love of God.

In these three Great Ones, whose nature is shining Love and Light, we can to some extent conceive of the essence of the nature of God. They are far greater than everything that is known of them or can be imagined. Human intelligence and aspiration can only faintly perceive their essential nature. Therefore, these qualities and energies must be transformed downwards. This lessening of tension for the purpose of transferring the energies further takes place at the May Full Moon each year. If we wish to partake together, we must be willing and endeavoring to transmit in an intelligible way the energies flowing into humanity on this day. It is therefore important to conceive of the esoteric truth just described and to dedicate ourselves to the service of the world in meditation.

It would be mistaken to wish to claim these energies and qualities only for oneself. In this way the flow would become dammed and would automatically fall prey to the laws of obstinacy, rigidity and decay which always carry destruction within them. The life continuing to flow in would accelerate the death of every crystallized form. We should therefore not resist the eternal stream of life pouring through us, we should not hold it up through desiring egoistically to have it for ourselves, but rather everything must remain in flux, must be transferred further. Therefore, the group as well as the individual turns in each meditation to the whole of humanity emitting to it in turn the energies which have flowed in.

This is particularly important at the Taurus Full Moon. We should activate our enthusiastic Will to take part in greater tasks than in the satisfaction of our personal desires alone. In this way, our own self-esteem grows to an increased extant. We should recognize that we can contribute a part—if only a very small one—in anchoring the forces of Light and Love on Earth. Each of us comprises a considerable part of the Great Whole; therefore, your contribution is just as important as mine. We wish to unite as a meditation group in order to attain the highest aspiration in the meditation.

Taurus Meditation

1. Stage: Preparation

During the meditation we sit with a straight back. We close our eyes, but may open them occasionally if tensions arise. We rest our hands on our thighs and place our feet together. We achieve the greatest relaxation of the body by transferring our inner focus to the middle of our body. We let the upper part of our body turn slightly in a circular motion until we have the sensation of sitting at the focal point, at the Hara.

The breath also has a part to play in the preparation for the meditation. We breathe in and out four times. On exhaling we say, "Let go—Relax", then we hold our breath and think "Become one", on inhaling "Become new", we hold our breath, "Be yourself". We do this a few times.

2. Stage: Alignment

Alignment of the threefold personality, physical, emotional and mental with the Soul. For this exercise in integration we use after every stage the Sacred Word OM in order to shut out all disruptive vibrations.

First of all the physical body. We are sitting calmly and quietly on our chair. We feel that we are borne by the chair, which is borne by the house, the house by the Earth, and the Earth by our planetary system. We open our physical body and dedicate it to the service of the Soul.

OM

The emotional body is relaxed and calm. We imagine to ourselves a motionless, sheet of blue water in which the Sun or the Moon is reflected. We feel love for all Mankind and dedicate our emotional body to its service.

OM

The mental body. Thoughts come and go. I remain quite calm listening into myself, looking at my thoughts, I do not let myself be distracted. I dedicate my thoughts to the good of Mankind, to the realization of the Divine Plan.

OM

Alignment With The Soul

Then I collect all the integrated powers of my personality into the innermost center of my Being. I stand fast like a rock, unshakeable at the nucleus, at the central point of my consciousness. At the nucleus I cannot be disturbed, having been attuned to a goal for ages. Nothing can throw me from my path. From this central power I shall create a new living space for myself, which is suited to my innermost Being and which gives expression to my Soul. I grow out of my inner potency into this space, slowly spreading out until I feel quite secure and calm.

3. Stage: Taurus Visualization Exercise

I am, utterly present, here on the chair, in this room, at this time, with these people.

I press against the chair and can feel the base of my spine. Then with my consciousness I very slowly slide up my spine. In so doing I imagine to myself the stem of a lotus blossom along which I am rising, between the small of my back, further up my back to my chest, quite slowly through the shoulder blades to base of my neck. There I stop.

Here a snow-white lotus blossom opens slowly and cautiously which has grown around my neck, covering my head. While this is taking place, I inaudibly hum the OM until the opened lotus blossom touches my shoulders.

I myself remain at the center, at the jewel of the lotus blossom, concentrating on my eyes. My eyelids are relaxed, vibrating lightly. I see and feel a white light flowing out from my forehead. It fills the room on all sides like a bright sea of light. It surrounds my head like a round ball, flowing at the same time out of my forehead once again and opening itself upwards.

We are receptive. We withdraw completely, opening ourselves upwards, allowing ourselves to be fertilized, influenced, illuminated.

Then we meditate on the Seed Thought of the sign Taurus:

I see, and when the Eye is opened, all is illumined.

4. Stage: Group Endeavor

We raise our consciousness to the highest point in our head, joining with all others who are approaching the spiritual energies in meditation at the time of the Full Moon. We form a group unity on the mental plane receptive to the cosmic energies which are now available. We behold a path of light stretching from humanity to Christ. In a valley in the Himalayas Christ receives the blessing of Buddha and passes it onto Mankind. We feel ourselves to be enclosed within His Love, dedicating the group to the service of the world.

We imagine how we all raise together a cup into the air in a highly concentrated inner aspiration, in an appeal to the spiritual powers of Light and Love which flow into our receptive consciousnesses and symbolically into the raised cup.

In the far distance in the dark blue night sky we see a point of light appear which is approaching us rapidly, becoming bigger and bigger, pouring its light into our cup. Everything around us is bathed in bright light.

5. Stage: Transmission To Humanity

We turn to humanity, allowing this living stream of the energy of Light, Love and creative Will to flow through us into the consciousness of Mankind and to spread itself. In so doing we imagine how these powers, spread out in numberless points of light and in a net of light over our planet, radiate penetrating all areas of our planetary life, so that these spiritual powers can effect the events of the world, everywhere and at all times.

We transfer the stream of energy together to humanity through the Great Invocation.

From the point of Light . . .
(see page 234)

OM OM OM

Completion Of The Meditation

We open our eyes inhaling and exhaling once deeply. We move our head, our neck, our shoulders, our feet, our hands. Then we extend to each other our hands, look into each other's eyes and bow before each other.

GEMINI

Notes • The festival of humanity • Christ Full Moon •
Process of transmission • Movement through space •
The Gemini Symbol • The planetary rulers •
The esoteric seed thought of Gemini •
Polarity: Gemini-Sagittarius, •
Axis of thought • Self-Knowledge •
The path of development of Gemini •
Hands and arms • Like attracts like •
Horizontal and vertical adjustment •
Awareness and synthesis • Place of meeting •
Alignment • The unifying factor •
Evaluation of the Gemini quality • Gemini Meditation •

GEMINI

GEMINI

Notes

Gemini	3rd sign of the Zodiac
Month	21 May-22 June
Cross	Mutable
Temperament	Air
Full Moon	Sun in Gemini Moon in Sagittarius
Houses	3rd House/9th House Axis of Thought
Problem Area	Collective intellectual norms— one's own view of the world
Planetary Rulers	exoterically Mercury esoterically Venus
Seed Thought	"I recognize my other Self and in the waning of that Self I grow and glow."

The Festival Of Humanity

Today we celebrate the Gemini Full Moon which is also called the "Festival of Humanity". It is the June festival dedicated above all to Christ and his relation to Mankind. According to Alice A. Bailey this festival comprises three days, each of which having a different leitmotif:

First Day: The motif of Love in its purest sense, free from sentiment, feeling or the wish to be loved. An understanding love which acts with firmness and decision and works for the whole (and not in the interests of a group or individual).

Second Day: The motif of the Resurrection, the new sort of life, of the living Christ-consciousness realized in us, of the power which makes all things new so that we can live "more to the full".

Third Day: The motif of Contact, of a closer relation between all Men of Good Will, between the cosmic quality of Love and Mankind.

Christ Full Moon

It has been delivered and symbolically represented to us how the energies let free during the Wesak Festival at the May Full Moon are poured out in a solemn ceremony on each of the three days by Christ to all Mankind. During these ceremonies the forces of Love, Light and Good Will are called upon in the "Great Invocation" and poured out to all those who took part in the great Wesak Festival for the purpose of creating a better world; through these the forces are transferred to the mass of humanity.

We can take part in the great process of transmission in today's Full Moon meditation by presenting as a group a receptive channel for these loving forces. We are called upon in a very special way for a great service, an invocation and a plea on behalf of Mankind, a plea for the pouring in of Light and Love into the decisions of Mankind so that correct human relations may be established.

Process of Transmission

And so we come to the special quality of the sign Gemini: the transmission of spiritual energies. It is a sign which creates relations demonstrating the common factor between pairs of opposites, the connecting factor. Mercury, the Ruler of this sign, is called "the Messenger of the Gods" in old myths "carrying messages to and fro with the speed of light between God and Mankind."

Movement Through Space

As you know, the sign Gemini belongs to the Mutable Cross. It represents so to speak the prototype of this Cross, whereas Taurus expresses the Fixed Cross most strongly and Aries the Cardinal. The impulse for the great process of transmission which takes place in Gemini was given in Aries. In Taurus the idea was perceived, received and clothed in the substance of the desire nature, that is, planted in the feeling body, and then in Gemini this energy enters the ethereal region, the mind of Man.

As a mutable air sign Gemini penetrates through simply everything. Therefore, the energies flow into the ramifications of all areas of life, into the manifoldness of appearances. Symbolically speaking, in Gemini the light perceived in Taurus is distributed to every single cell of the body. From the esoteric point of view this process is therefore concerned with the transfiguration of the personality.

In addition, the time dimension also starts to develop with Gemini. Space and time meet here. As we may remember, we created a space for ourselves in Taurus. In Gemini we can move through this space. The Geminian cannot remain still in one place; he goes to the nearest, objective thing and studies it; he wants to know more about it, how it is constructed, what it is made of. By moving through space we also discover people and realize that we are not alone. Neighbors, brothers and sisters, relatives and acquaintances are near us. We go to them; we meet them and learn something from them.

We can learn a lot if we accept into ourselves our environment with an alert consciousness and an active intelligence. In the Gemini month we collect information and realizations. We can also learn something about ourselves however. We can ask ourselves, "What do other people think about me? How do they judge my behavior?" One can also encounter oneself.

The Gemini Symbol ♊

The symbol of the sign Gemini shows a bowl at its top and bottom which are connected by two vertical lines; one vertical symbolizes the condition of personality and represents the "Ego-rune". Two vertical lines symbolize a twofold condition of personality, double nature. It is the "two souls within my breast", as is so often sung.

It is difficult to penetrate the real, deep Being of a Gemini because he often shows himself other than he really is. What enables him to appear adroit, adaptable and diplomatic on the one hand, can be expressed on the other as something shrewd and crafty in the character. His main problem is therefore duality and variety. These are also the trials on the spiritual path. He can only too easily become lost in the variety of the forms of the world, and then he can no longer distinguish differences in value. Many things which are different in quality are considered to be equal, and the true proportion or relationship to other differences in value are no longer taken into account. Thus, the inner and more valuable significance of a thing or of a person or of an opinion is often overlooked.

This is similarly expressed by the Gemini symbol. The upper, open bowl represents pictorially the receptive principle. Everything is received—material or spiritual, good or bad, valuable or valueless. Everything penetrates through the bowl being filtered at the same time through the personality, through the Ego and passed on to the surrounding world. The emission of forces, knowledge and qualities is symbolized by the lower bowl. It is the great principle of transmission of which we spoke at the beginning. The Mutable Cross, the Air element, as well as the mental agility of the Ruler Mercury make this possible. Transmission is one of the most important abilities, but also one of the greatest difficulties of the sign.

The Planetary Rulers ☿ ♀

Mercury, as the principle of transmission, brings the relation between the two poles of personality, Soul and Ego, into an active stage of encounter. The esoteric Ruler of Gemini is Venus who resolves the duality with her unifying quality and transforms it into a "fluid synthesis", as it is expressed esoterically. The fusion of the pairs of polar opposites occurs in the consciousness through Love which embraces everything. The spiritually striving Geminian must concern himself with this synthesis of opposites and for the reconciliation between himself and others. The agility of Mercury must combine with the wisdom and feeling for value of Venus; in this way the ability will be developed of comprehending extremes and of combining them in a higher way. Mercury, as the arbiter between the higher and the lower mind, produces the differentiation between the Self and the Non-Self, between Soul and personality, between EGO and YOU.

The Esoteric Seed Thought Of Gemini Runs

I recognize my other Self and in the waning of that Self I grow and glow.

For the consciously striving individual Venus will increasingly appear as the esoteric Ruler. Venus assists in making the right choice from so many possibilities and from the confusing variety of things. In the Gemini month we can learn to be satisfied with what is ours, with what is important and what corresponds to our innermost Being. We must not let ourselves be distracted by the many things which enter our consciousness, but must adjust ourselves to that which is important and which suits us. We must first however find this out by first of all examining with Mercury all possibilities and by collecting together everything worth knowing. With the assistance of Venus we can recognize the inner quality of an object or of a person and concentrate our love on the essential, the valuable. We can make the right joice, decide with certainty and aim our powers at the goal.

Polarity: Gemini-Sagittarius
Axis Of Thought

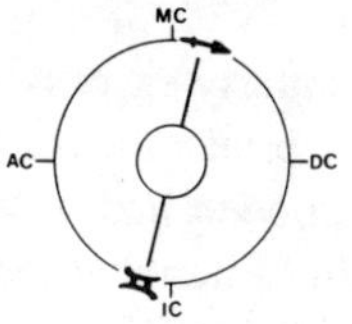

In this process of struggling for the real and the essential the opposite sign Sagittarius becomes active. In the polarity of the extraneous and the inherent the Geminian is continually going through the experience of duality, during which he is thrown to and fro by doubt and confidence.

From time to time common sense gets the upper hand over feeling, and from time to time the intellect is stronger than the emotions. This causes some imbalance and some disunity to arise in his Being, in his appearance and in his manner. One moment elated, the next dejected is characteristic of his mood; today full of believing optimism, tomorrow once again full of dejected indecisiveness. Fortunately, both types of mood do not last long as the essence of the Geminian is too active, too adaptable and too dependent on ever changing impressions. He always needs people around him, and it is difficult for him to be alone. He needs activity, movement and bustle; he cannot sit still, and he would prefer to be in many places at once.

The spiritual way to the true Self however demands that he reverts to and contemplates on the real, on his inner direction, the correct orientation and goal setting hidden in the opposite sign Sagittarius. The sources of pure spiritual force must not be sought in the outer world among important and influential personalities or from what some authority or institution has said or from what he may have read in a book but within his own inner Self. This searching for real meaning and purpose characterizes the life of the spiritually orientated Gemini.

The duality often also leads him in wrong directions. He finds false values; he considers all things to be of equal importance losing his sense of proportion and dedicating himself to false things or people who possess more outwardly than within and whom he tries to imitate for a long time without noticing it. On the other hand, he often assesses himself wrongly, fooling himself until he notices that he is not on the right track. In this way self-experience, the recognition of the true Self, is restricted. One is always inclined to constantly justify oneself, to believe that one is right. Thus, the negative spirit of Sagittarius takes effect, or "cold positivism" which serves as a defense against feelings of guilt. Within however he cannot fool himself to such an extent that he does not know who or what he is.

In the Gemini month we all more or less have to struggle with this polarity. As soon as we start to fool ourselves, trying to hide ourselves from others, we also conceal ourselves behind our own pretense. In the encounter with others one then fears possible rejection, being excluded. As a Geminian however one wants to be present everywhere. The Geminian would like to be accepted, recognized and loved. Yet it is in this very association with the world that the portion of Being representing his inner reality remains frequently hidden—at least, so long as he believes that he must direct himself according to others or to a current opinion. As soon as he has realized however that there are other possibilities than those postulated by collective norms or determined by currents of fashion, he begins to trust his own mind and his own capacity for judgement.

Self-Knowledge

In this respect he requires the courage for self-knowledge, which means that one must stand apart, at least for a time, from the apparently secure Collective Mind in order to be able to go one's own way. Here the Geminian is often overcome by the worry of whether he may really do this, whether he really can do it. This does not last long however, for curiosity allows him to forget his worries again more or less quickly.

We are all faced with this problem of struggling with the real, with true self-knowledge. At certain moments we recognize ourselves for what we are. Then we are shocked, perhaps in a way similar to the shock when we hear our own voice for the first time on tape. Frequently we often sound strange and unknown to ourselves because we believe we are what upbringing has made of us: that well-adjusted human child with a certain type of behavior. We then recognize that we are only "adjusted" and perhaps far removed from our real inner Being. We recognize that all our amassed knowledge does not lead to self-knowledge, but is only a lamentable attempt to avoid, in an intellectual way, the painful recognition that our existence does not agree with knowledge. Self-experience only becomes possible when we expose ourselves, when we dare to step aside from collective norms of thinking, from prescribed modes of behavior, then the opposite sign Sagittarius takes effect. This however requires the courage to brush aside the imcompatible mask or conditioned mode of behavior. Especially the Geminian identifies himself too easily, due to insecurity or inner immaturity, with that which impinges itself on him, with the impressions, with the opinions and knowledge of other people. He believes that he is all this himself. Thus, it slides slowly into self-alientation; he lives in his so-called "apparent Ego" representing his other Self which he must recognize as something outside his own inner Being and often having nothing to do with his real essence. Once the process of distancing and freeing himself from this has started, then this "apparent Ego" disappears. His own Self grows and shines in genuine glory, as stated in the Seed Thought. In order to become himself completely, he must therefore free himself from the functions of the collective Superego, recognizing this to be something incompatible with his nature.

The Path Of Development Of Gemini

Only in this way will the Geminian become the transmitter of pure spiritual qualities. If he is in contact with his inner source, he will become useful as a transmitter, as a mediator. Esoterically it is the synthesis between sober understanding and highest spiritual Love which he is striving for and which frees him from his duality and his inner division and leads him towards intuition and pure reason. Pure reason, as we have been told, is the most perfect form of Love. But the path to the achievement of this goal is characterized by conflicts, mistakes, criticism, errors and extraneous influences.

Conflict is also the esoteric-psychological element for further development. Harmony through conflict is the path for the sign Gemini. The conflict arises through the opposition of pairs of opposites and the harmony through the fusion with the innermost kernel of Being, the Soul.

In the sign Gemini the spiritually striving person can learn to a certain extent to understand correctly what we call the "mechanism of recognition" and simultaneously understand those processes of life which enable a person to at last be what he really is. Through his ability to turn intellectually in any direction with ease and to differentiate between the many objects in the physical world and to order them correctly, the Messenger of the Gods appears in his true nature, capable of combining extremes together in a higher way.

Hands And Arms

As is well known, the hands and arms are ruled by Gemini. If we take this as a symbol, then we always need both hands or both sides of our Being when we are at work and when we are mentally active. The left hand always seconds and supports the right; they work in contrast and not in opposition. It is exactly the same with the objects within ourselves, between Man and his environment, Soul and personality. It is a matter of the completion, the penetration, the rounding off of our Being. Through the integration of the threefold personality the balance, the center, is achieved and maintained; the duality or division disappears and Man arrives at a synthesis, at wholeness.

Like Attracts Like

In his consciousness everyone can combine everything with everything else, co-ordinate or integrate himself. This can only succeed however when the same vibration exists, for like only attracts like. The same degree of vibration can cause uniformed, similarly directed behavior, as one finds it in the Collective Mind, but it also activates the capacity for adaption, the "fluid synthesis" of Venus. Venus as a selective mechanism attracts what is suitable to her. If we tune ourselves in to her, we shall be led where we can find what we need and where we shall find what is in harmony with us or what will advance us a little further. We are therefore always present and adjusted to the moment, ready to move, waiting for the right opportunity to be able to attune ourselves.

The process of co-ordination is twofold, as indeed everything in Gemini is subject to duality. Either we step out into the world gathering everything possible together in the hope that it may help us, or we are secure and firm within ourselves, confidently knowing that what belongs to us will be joined or has been joined to us through Love. It is good practice if we let things pass us by, waiting for the object or the people we need to enter our field of vision and to whom we have something to say or to transmit.

Horizontal And Vertical Adjustment

There are therefore constantly two forms of behavior in Gemini. The horizontal form in which he projects himself and his wishes outwards living without personal bounds, and the way inwards by which he knows what he wants, only seeking and using that in particular which is really important and essential and which can help many other people in their efforts to attain spiritual growth.

In horizontal development we always seek the same thing, confirmation in the outside world, for the sake of security when we are full of doubt about ourselves and about the truth. In vertical development we adjust ourselves according to what we have realized and experienced. Thus we come to a synthesis, a wholeness, and summon the qualities of the opposite sign Sagittarius.

For the attainment of this wholeness, we should make the effort to draw back into ourselves those powers which strive outwards into diversity. Just as thankfulness was a help to us in Taurus, so in Gemini it is the confidence and the knowledge that we have done everything, that we have attained all possible knowledge to prepare us for the higher recognition, for the inner Light which comes from our true Self.

If we were to continue to collect and appropriate knowledge which we could neither evaluate nor order, then the world would become a mathematical sum for us—and what would that profit us? Therefore, we must withdraw within ourselves in the confidence that we must now learn to wait until what we have appropriated becomes mature and effective. We know that our action and all our endeavors will bear fruit which we shall come to enjoy if we adopt "reception stations".

In this way we adjust ourselves horizontally instead of vertically. We look upwards and wait. All forces pushing hectically outwards become calm. We know that we need not do anything further because we have already done everything that needs to be done and because we are well prepared. We know that our efforts and our actions will cause an effect, and we wait. "I shall meet you half way" runs the saying. This is the law of invocation and evocation which in reality sets the great principle of transmission in movement and which is used during meditation. We must learn to listen to our inner Being, but also to our environment; with all our senses we must pay attention to our intuitive direction so that we are aware at the right moment of the transmission of energy and of the inspiration, fully prepared to accept the blessing, the knowledge or the message.

Awareness And Synthesis

We must also cultivate in our lives this attitude of awareness, of being fully present. The inner adjustment and co-ordination with our intuitive direction will always enable us to be at the right place at the right time. This is well known to be the "timing" of the person successful in life. It is the combination of supply and demand, of outer opportunities and inner requirements, as well as the pleasing occurrence of genuine meetings between human beings.

In the mutable sign Gemini active processes are therefore always taking place. Something is always on the move or always taking place. Nothing here is static or firmly ordained. It is a dynamic adjustment which must first be achieved.

Place of Meeting

We all know here in our group that at the Taurus Full Moon the Buddha passed on his blessing to Christ. Now in the sign Gemini a further transmission takes place: the enlightenment, the message and the blessing are passed on further to Mankind. This message will flow in and be transmitted to the variety of human consciousness, to the mass and to the Collective Mind. Today we can partake consciously in it.

In the Gemini meditation it is important to know that we must place ourselves at the same vibration, proceed inwardly to the place where the transmission of energy will take place. Once we have found the right people, then we set out on the way to them to meet them. Similarly, in the meditation we must raise our consciousness to the plane where the transmission or the meeting or the exchange will take place. This is in reality the alignment which we must always make before each meditation. It is always important that we find each other, that we meet, are there at the right time and prepared for what is going to take place. In this way we unite opposites, the duality. This meeting place, this co-ordination is important. Today we want to make the effort to reach this place of exchange together inwardly in our consciousness in order to be able to take part in the transmission of energy, Light and Love.

Alignment

Just to recapitulate: alignment always takes place vertically and horizontally. We reach the outer world by recognizing our fellow men and all the many who are still present. We join with them in love accepting them as brothers and sisters and align ourselves in the knowledge that "I am a human being like these." Then we raise our consciousness, vertically, and know that our Soul, our higher Self is also looking for us wanting to join with us. The Soul has set out, just as much as we have, to find and meet us. The meeting can take place in Gemini, for here we recognize our other Self; here we meet ourselves. The duality becomes a fluid synthesis because the meeting and the co-ordination cause an exchange, a contact, a pressing of hands.

"By recognizing my other Self, I grow and glow"—refers to this process. The other Self disappears as its substance flows over into us and we ourselves become inner illumination.

The Unifying Factor

In human life the exchange, the co-ordination takes place when we grow beyond the contrast between good and bad and find the unifying, harmonious factor, the meaning. It requires self-control, uninterrupted effort and the cultivation of the gift for differentiation, of wisdom in order that the good and the meaningful may be found even in the apparently worst situations and to create a functional, self-perfecting unity out of contrasts. As two lovers approach each other, penetrate each other in order to become one, so the contrasts in Man must be perfected, rounded off, even be in love with each other, which is described in spiritual literature as a "mystical marriage" or as the Third Initiation of the Transfiguration. And we can experience this within ourselves through the influence of the Gemini quality.

Once we have become one in this way with the essential, then we shall also be able to detect the true Self behind each person. Our recognition and our love will flow out instinctively to him. This happens through the unifying inner Self which is one with all in the sense, "All the Sons of Man are one at heart."

Evaluation Of The Gemini Quality

Wherever we have become obstinately attached to an idea, an opinion, to suffering or isolation, the relating spirit of the sign Gemini can help us above all in the month to see things in another way for once. The Geminian always sees two or more sides to a thing. That can be curing and helpful, above all for those who view themselves as the dramatic center of their world and fall at every occasion into tragic doubt. The Geminian knows that every coin has a reverse side and that something positive is to be found in all things. He will always emphasize this, thus helping to establish balance in the world again.

Therefore, a special opportunity presents itself to us today, of considering what has happened to us from another angle. Thus, we can perhaps exercise more tolerance towards those who have done us wrong. We can reconcile ourselves with them and forgive them, instigating a discussion and establishing peace again.

The Gemini quality flowing down to us enables us today through its adaptability and fluidity to clear away crystallized states of affairs, to settle old accounts, to put right mistakes and to begin anew in the sense, "Behold, I make all things new." In this way we join with the all-loving spirit of Christ with the benevolent understanding which is common to all mutable signs—Gemini, Virgo, Sagittarius and Pisces. Gemini as well can understand everything, not only through Mercury but also through Venus. Gemini recognizes the manifoldness of all things and recognizes that not everything can be bad all the time.

An old wise saying runs, "the more one knows, the less one can judge." We wish to join today at the Gemini Full Moon with this all-understanding, lovingly understanding Gemini spirit radiating it out to all people with whom we come in contact.

We wish to awaken the powers of Good Will with a request for enlightenment and understanding for those everywhere who have to make decisions for humanity.

In so doing the practical success of this spiritual effort depends on the ability to increase the Light and Love we already possess, to understand others better and to spread Good Will in order to establish correct human relations in the family and in the group.

First of all today we shall practice a meditative exercise in horizontal and vertical identification corresponding to the duality of the sign Gemini, uniting the two halves of Being where these two lines cross or are co-ordinated at the focal point of Being, at the center of the cross.

Gemini Meditation

1. Stage: Preparation

During the meditation we sit with a straight back. We close our eyes, but may open them occasionally if tensions arise. We rest our hands on our thighs and place our feet together. We achieve the greatest relaxation of the body by transferring our inner focus to the middle of our body. We let the upper part of our body turn slightly in a circular motion until we have the sensation of sitting at the focal point, at the Hara.

The breath also has a part to play in the preparation for the meditation. We breathe in and out four times. On exhaling we say "Let go—Relax", then we hold our breath for "Become one". We breathe a "Become new", and on holding the breath "Be yourself". The "Let go" comprises all our worries, anxieties, tensions and agitation. The "Relax" is the trusting of ourselves to the fundamental healing powers within. In the "Become one" we surrender ourselves to the real, the original, the Self. In the "Become new" new powers flow into us, and in the "Be yourself" we concentrate these powers within our Ego. We do this a few times.

2. Stage: Alignment

Alignment of the threefold personality, physical, emotional and mental with the Soul. For this exercise in integration we use after every stage and Sacred Word OM in order to shut out all disruptive vibrations.

a) The Physical Body
We pump some air into our lower body, maintaining the physical focal point at the Hara and identifying with the physical body.

I am here, fully present, here on this chair, in this room, at this hour, with these people. I am sitting on the chair, the chair is borne by the house, the house by the Earth, the Earth by the planet, the planet is borne by the cosmic laws of gravity. This conformity secures my life. I am supported, secure. I extend my consciousness, beholding the Earth, the horizon and the whole sphere of the planet. My body is a part of the Earth, of this planet; after death I shall return to the Earth, yet I shall remain.

I dedicate my physical body to heightened perception and to the service of the Soul.

b) The Emotional Body
I concentrate on the heart center. I have an emotional body with desires—desires for love, understanding, peace, happiness. My neighbor has the same desires, feelings; I can extend my emotional body to my fellow men, to my family, to the group, to the town in which I live, to the whole nation in which I live.

I expand my emotional body further out over the borders of my nation to other nations. They are all human beings like you and I. I can see the people in America, in Europe, in Russia, in China, in Africa; they are all human beings like myself. I identify in love with all humanity of which I am but a tiny part. I dedicate my emotional body to involvement with mankind.

c) The Mental Body
Then I raise my consciousness into my head, first of all into the center of the brain and then into the center between thc cyebrows. My eyelids are relaxed. I

can see thoughts slipping through my brain; they come from all directions; they are all around me; they penetrate me, an uninterrupted stream of thought. Yet I remain at the center and observe them; I look on them as playing children.

I, the focus of consciousness, the I AM on the mental plane, can direct my thoughts through my own Will. I have the freedom of only thinking what is good for me and for all humanity. I only think positive, edifying thoughts dedicating the increase in my capacity for realization to the Plan of evolution.

OM

d) The Causal Or Soul Body

I free myself from all thoughts surrounding me drawing all forces back within me. I penetrate even deeper within myself, drawing everything in to the central point, to the center of the brain and raising my consciousness to the highest point in my head. I am the Soul. As a Soul I let an inaudible OM sound and breathe Light, understanding and Love into the waiting, attentative and integrated personality.

3. Stage: Gemini Visualization Exercise

I support the process by imagining a golden-white shining Sun situated behind me. It slowly expands becoming larger and penetrating my expectant personality, enveloping me completely, taking me up in its light.

I recognize my other Self and in the waning of that Self I grow and glow.

4. Stage: Group Endeavor

We stand as a group unity on the mental plane receptive to the cosmic Gemini energies. We behold a path of light stretching from humanity to that source where the Love of God dwells, which is expressed on this planet through Christ. We feel ourselves to be enclosed within this Love and dedicate the group in the great process of transmission to the service of the world.

We extend our consciousness to our group and join with all those who approach the Full Moon energies in meditation. In our vision the Sun becomes larger enclosing all those joined with us in its light.

We imagine how we all raise together a cup into the air in a highly concentrated inner aspiration, in an appeal to the spiritual powers of Light and Love which flow into our receptive consciousnessness—symbolically into the raised cup. We raise our hands very slowly:

> Oh, Thou in whom we live, breathe and have our being, the power which makes all things new, turn the fate of Men to better things, everywhere move the hearts of Men so that they may open themselves to the spirit of love and brotherhood and mutual responsibility.

May the Will for Good be the motive of all deeds and may it establish once again the reign of peace on Earth.

May the love of the devine Self be shed abroad in our heart, through our group and throughout the world.

5. Stage: Transmission To Humanity

We turn to humanity, allowing this living stream of the energy of Light, Love and creative Will to flow through us into the consciousness of Mankind and to spread itself. In so doing we imagine how these powers are caught up by numberless points of light and spread out like a net of light over our whole planet; how they radiate, penetrating all areas of our planetary life, so that these spiritual powers can effect the events of the world, everywhere and at all times.

We transfer the stream of energy together to humanity through the Great Invocation.

From the point of Light...
(see page 234)

OM OM OM

Completion Of The Meditation

We open our eyes inhaling and exhaling once deeply. We move our head, our neck, our shoulders, our feet, our hands. Then we extend to each other our hands, look into each other's eyes and bow before each other.

CANCER

Notes • Process of manifestation • Collective sign •
The law of the Avaters • The planetary rulers •
The esoteric seed thought of cancer •
The symbol of Cancer • Polarity: Cancer-Capricorn,
Axis of Individuality •
The way to the source • The tree as an example •
Contradiction and uncertainty •
Birth crises and anxieties • Conquering the past •
Rooted in one's own being • Cancer Meditation •

CANCER

CANCER

Notes

Cancer	4th sign of the Zodiac
Month	22 June–22 July
Cross	Cardinal
Temperament	Water
Full Moon	Sun in Cancer Moon in Capricorn
Houses	4th House/10th House Axis of Individuality
Problem Area	Opposition: Collective—Individual
Planetary Rulers	exoterically Moon esoterically Neptune
Seed Thought	"I build a lighted house and therein dwell."

Process of Manifestation

As you will remember, in Aries we began to form an idea with which the process of manifestation was initiated. This idea came through Aries into the human brain, into the head. In Taurus this idea reached the emotional or desire body. It was given substance by the power of desire and enveloped in an astral form. In the sign Gemini the idea reached the ethereal area of human life, the multitude of forms and cognitions. In Cancer this idea, thought or energy from the abstract area of ideas now receives a physical form.

This process of transmitting downwards has an analogy in the human constitution and development. In Aries the mental or thinking body is developed, in Taurus the desire or feeling body and in Gemini the ethereal body or life body. In Cancer this process takes on firm physical form. Here we are dealing with the integration of the personality in its threefold expression which will then become a unity in Leo.

According to "Esoteric Astrology" by Alice A. Bailey, Cancer is the Door to Manifestation in which the Soul takes on a firm body. Here the form, the personality is born, completed and at the same time begins at the IC the ascent to conscious individuality in Capricorn, its opposite sign.

With the sign Cancer we have reached the deepest point in the circle of the Zodiac. It is therefore also the access point to the Collective Unconscious, to the archetypal region and to our deepest layers of Being, to our Self through which we are connected with everything living. Plunging into the Collective Unconscious can lead us to become one with the great Being from whom we receive our life. It is the condition of recognizing our primal source where we recognize the Self as One and receive the power which makes all things new. Expressed in other words, the attainment of an identical condition of vibration with the Being of all things, whereby we experience equality and unity with the Self and with other human beings.

Collective Sign

Cancer is the sign of membership of a Collective, of a group, of a family. Through identical vibration we receive new power and attain a new vitalizing dimension of membership, security and unity. We realize—for example in our meditation group—that we are all animated by the same ideal, by the same spirit and that we receive our power to keep going from this identical vibration.

Collective force is identical vibration, group consciousness is similarly identical vibration. The former is unconscious, the latter presupposes consciousness. Group consciousness is a conformity which one only experiences when as an individual united with the group spirit one provides a service in the world giving the Collective new direction and fecundating anew the Collective Spirit—making all things new.

Identical vibration can be achieved here either horizontally or vertically. Horizontally it is achieved with the group, vertically with our own Self.

The Law Of The Avatars

To a certain extent this is also the Law of the Avatars. Avatars are Beings who either, coming from above from the spiritual plane, illuminate the minds of Men or, coming from the people, from the Collective, formulate the necessary changes in the Collective and bring it to manifestation.

According to esoteric tradition, the spiritual Avatars are intelligent, superior Beings who in deep meditation by force of there capacity of mind perceive a new world creating new forms of thought, new ideals which are taken up by humanity and towards whom they can be orientated.

As human beings we can imitate this process in turn, continuously repeating it consciously or unconsciously. We create thought forms clothing them in astral material, that is, the idea which we have or perceive is fed and vitalized by our power of desire without letting us go until it has become reality. Every superficial or visible idea therefore possesses a form animated by longing and created from the power of thought.

The capacity of thought impresses the perceived ideas onto the level of feeling, into the desire nature in order to thus elicit the "incarnated idea" for the purpose of clothing it in a form. This level of feeling is particularly active in Cancer (that feminine, watery sign) and can therefore be described as it were as the basis for pregnancy. Therefore, this period is also similar to the stage of conception, which passively waiting allows itself to be impressed by the spirit.

The Planetary Rulers ☽ ♆

People born under Cancer are very impressionable, they are continuously subject to humor and moods because they are subject to a special extent to the Moon and its phases. Sensations and feelings play an important role in this. A typical characteristic is the strong sensibility, even sensitivity with which a Cancerian reacts rapidly and intensively to the people around him.

In Cancer the Moon rules exoterically over the form nature and Neptune esoterically over the consciousness. The Moon makes an emotional person of the Cancerian, with a strong need for dependence and with the longing to always have someone to whom he can open his feelings or whom he can protect with them. He is therefore very dependent on the Collective surrounding him, be this his family or the environment in a wider sense. The Moon makes of him a person of the Collective or of the mass, whereas Neptune makes him receptive to higher impressions enabling him to take on tasks for the whole community because he understands this well and is a part of it. This does not mean however being pleasant to everyone at any price, but rather helping other people in a spiritual sense, that is, to serve them knowingly. That is a great difference, offering the Cancerian a direct path to his own Self.

It is therefore a matter for Cancerians of overcoming mass consciousness and dependence on the Collective and of expanding into the Universal Consciousness of Neptune, of Universal Love and universal bonds.

The Esoteric Seed Thought Of Cancer Runs:

I build a lighted house and therein dwell.

The house built by Cancer must be bright and lighted, no dark dungeon. If it is lit by the Universal Love for humanity of Neptune, then it will attract everything around it through its light and warmth, and the Cancerian will no longer be alone. If his house is dark however, he will have to suffer loneliness and complete isolation. Therefore, the Cancerian should give up his egoism and conquer his small, security-conscious Moon-Ego in order to be able to partake of the unifying force of Divine Love in Neptune. Through the sensitive planets Moon and Neptune, hope and expectation, longing and desire pass through his life incessantly.

The Symbol Of Cancer ♋

This inner characteristic is also shown in the symbol of Cancer. It presents two bowls merging into an open circle through which everything can flow. The upper bowl shows movement to the left representing a step backwards, a striving towards the starting point, the source of life, the beginning of existence. The lower bowl shows movement from left to right representing a step out into the world in order to prove oneself there and the realize oneself. These two forces of stepping out into the world and of withdrawing into one's own being continue in a constant rhythm corresponding to the Cardinal phases of impulse and relaxation. This also corresponds to the pulse beat of life, inhaling and exhaling, death and rebirth.

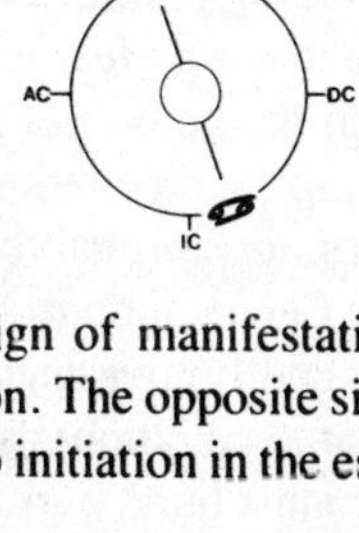

Polarity: Cancer-Capricorn
Axis of Individuality

As has already been said, Cancer is the sign of manifestation, the door through which the Soul can enter into incarnation. The opposite sign Capricorn is the sign of individualization and is the door to initiation in the esoteric sense, and to individualization in the psychological.

The sign Cancer as the sign of collective dependence, of the herd instinct is thus the polar opposite of the condition of individual consciousness. The difference between mass-consciousness and individual consciousness is to be seen here. Many people are standing today at the dividing of the ways between these two states of consciousness. The theme of the Collective and the individual is therefore occupying many great thinkers of our epoch.

Essentially, Cancer is about the realization that this sign is one of the two doors of the Zodiac through which the Soul enters into the outer physical world taking on a form with which it then identifies throughout many cycles. It is "the gate which stands wide open, broad and easy to pass through", as it is expressed in the Old Commentary.

This door is associated with material nature, with the mother of form, just as the other door, Capricorn, is associated with the spirit, "the father of everything that is". It is therefore the great tension between spirit and matter, between father and mother, collective and individual with which we are concerned today. A way leads down to the mothers, to the source of life, another upwards to conscious, autonomous individuality.

The Way To The Source

If we follow the movement inwards, we shall find our source hidden deep within us. Here is the beginning of individual development. At the source we can discover the roots of our Being. But we only arrive at the source when we swim against the current—and that always requires the dissociation of ourselves from collective dependence, a step outwards from the security of our safe nest in order to become an independent individual.

At the source lies the cause of our life, of our prospering, but also of our worries and difficulties. During the Cancer month we can find the roots, the cause or the source. Now we can undertake the necessary corrections so that our character, our physical and spiritual form can become as perfect as possible. In this way we increasingly resemble the inner image which is already present here at the root of our Being, in the seed or kernel. We wish to trace this kernel, this germ of our Being. We shall then be confronted with ourselves as we were conceived in the beginning, as we were created by the Creator perfect in spirit. We recognize that a perfect form lives within us, a likeness of inner divinity, even if only in the germ, yet as an inner potency which we are to discover.

Today during the meditation we shall do an exercise for the transparency or permeability of our spiritual form, of our threefold personality. As has already been said, the Cancer month is concerned with a vessel, with the development of our various bodily coverings, with the integration of the personality so that it receives the same vibrations as the Soul. In accordance with the Seed Thought of Cancer we must build ourselves a lighted house, that is, our spiritual body must become healthy, our feelings full of love and our thoughts directed towards good. This assimilation is a process of growth which takes place everywhere.

The Tree As An Example

In life growth occurs on account of forces which effect us from within and without. In the plant kingdom we can observe this process in the seed of a tree. In a single acorn everything is contained which will finally appear as a great mighty oak. In order to attain its full growth, the seed must have suitable soil; it sustains itself from the substance of the soil and from the activity of the Sun and rain. When it begins to grow to the light of day, it is strengthened by the wind. This miracle of the unfolding of that which was within it cannot take place unless the indwelling ability is present on which the forces from without may work positively.

When a human being reacts correctly to the impulse of the influences coming from without and to the inner voice of his heart, then he will progress stage by stage through perceptions to complete self-realization—the inner and the outer will have become a unity.

Let us remain with the example of the tree, then we can also imagine in the sign Cancer, the deepest point in the Zodiac. The tree of life whose roots reach deep down into the firmness of the Earth. In this tree sit the three Fates spinning the web of fate, as is passed down to us in sagas and legends. This is an indication that fate begins at the roots, at the source; there the cause of the process of life is placed. In Cancer the germ, the seed of life is already present which drives us onwards on the ladder to individualization. It is the secret power of development, of evolution and is concerned, as in every Cardinal sign, with the Will. Here in Cancer the personal Will becomes aware of itself for the first time. One already feels that one wants to climb to the summit, to Capricorn. This individual Will awakes like a germ in the sign Cancer.

Contradictions And Uncertainty

Therefore, Cancer is a contradictory sign. On the one hand one wants to remain a child fleeing to the security of family life, the Collective or the apron strings of mother. One is anxious about the world and its possible dangers, but nevertheless the movement towards individual freedom, to independent action has already begun, which causes the first disassociation from the maternal or family ties. Therefore, the Cancerian is often thrown to and fro. The conflict between holding fast to the security of the home and the urge to the wide world makes him moody, unpredictable, insecure. For here the ways part; it is a real fork in the road and one frequently does not know which way to take. This inner insecurity makes the Cancerian susceptible to the influences of his surroundings.

If he cannot make up his mind, remaining undecided for a long time, he becomes the victim of his own instinctive and emotional forces without the freedom of decision. He then blindly follows the general current obeying the orders of others and being easily influenced. This insecurity and formlessness are reflected in his life; he easily falls under the influence of common opinions and collective norms and can be led by the strong Will of another. He becomes an individual of the mass and suffers from the inability to shape his own world. As long as he lacks the form to give his own Being expression, he suffers from being misunderstood in his inner Being. Therefore, the integration of the personality must be started in Cancer and one's own Will developed.

Birth Crises And Anxieties

Cancer is the birth place of the individual person who from his own Free Will and ability takes a road which leads him away from behavior according to collective norms to the independent personality in Leo. As with every other birth, this process is accompanied by pains, crises, anxieties, inner needs and varying emotional states. Here the anxiety of being handed over unprotected to the world plays a considerable role. Therefore, in Cancer one must build a house in which one can live, or attain a firm form of personality which is equal to the demands of life. By the house is meant a firm form which offers the necessary protection against the injustices of nature. Hither one can rush when it is stormy outside and dangerous, here new power and new courage can be created to master the many tasks of life. Each human being needs this protection.

In the case of unprocessed experiences the anxiety in the face of the world is so great that the natural affairs of life become to be regarded as unbridgeable difficulties. One no longer dares to go out but stays sitting, alone and isolated, within one's four walls because one only feels secure in one's own house, within oneself. This can go so far that one barricades oneself in, hindering further growth.

Conquering The Past

Unpleasant experiences, terrifying impressions from childhood establish themselves in Cancer, are taken up into the fountain of memory and can become a hinderance for every vital experience. Therefore, the Cancerian must learn to get the better of memories from the past, failures and bitter disappointments. If he depends to much on the past, looking continuously backwards, then he will turn to a pillar of salt like Lot's wife; he gets stuck and cannot find the way to his own living source and to his individual development.

In the Cancer month we all have the opportunity to clear out the past forgetting the things that lie behind us and turning to our new spiritual opportunities. We must look forward, seizing hold of confidence and courage, striving on full of faithful optimism. This can best be accomplished by turning in to our depths and making contact with the soil of Being unconnected with all outer dangers.

Rooted In One's Own Being

Once we have become rooted in our own Being, we can experience feelings of security and of the self-evident protection of life. Just as a child we ran to mother when we were hungry, when we were dirty or when someone had annoyed us, so we can dive down into our own depths coming into contact there with the concealing forces of the maternal womb and creating new power. Being rooted in one's own Being is like being fixed in a deeper soil where we can settle down full of confidence experiencing and withstanding the world without anxiety. Here we experience being one and have a share in the supportive and concealing forces of communal life. In being one with one's Being many problems solve themselves as if by magic. We penetrate a dimension where other laws apply. We feel as if we have been caught up by a higher power and Love which are not of this world. When we abandon ourselves to the inner, ordering forces of our own Self, then the inner and outer world is transformed accordingly.

From these depths the inner Light is also nourished and fed, the Light which arises from security, from being one with one's Self. Then our house will be lighted so that others can find the way to warm themselves in the protecting security of the maternal, domestic hearth. Just as we nourish ourselves from our own depths, now we can nourish all those who come to us asking for help, love and understanding.

We can therefore learn during the Cancer month to give protection and security to other people too by bringing love to unfoldment and by taking care of someone or something, fostering and protecting it from dangers. Thus, we develop our best Cancer qualities, for we all have these qualities in us. Then we, our house and our dwelling place will become a place to which others gladly come because they feel comfortable and secure there and can create new power. If on the other hand we cut ourselves off on account of some anxiety or other, then we are separated from the vital stream of life sitting a captive of our own Ego-form and unable to grow further or to fulfill our task in life.

We should become ever more capable of helping others or of doing them a service. This attitude should become a constant inner drive, a fundamental motivation in itself. In this way even in daily life we shall be constantly in harmony with our inner powers of Being and live, work and love with all creation.

Even our Zodiac meditation is in reality a service. It is a question of coming into contact with the special qualities of the corresponding month evaluating these positively in our life and passing them on to other people in our vicinity. Through our group meditation we erect to a certain extent a channel made of the material of mind by which the qualities flow down and can be brought into the consciousness of humanity.

Thought represents an energy which we can apply accordingly in order to create a new structure for our Being which meets the demands of our inner Being. "Energy follows thought" and "as a man thinks in his heart, thus he is". Everything that takes place on Earth is born first in the region of the spirit. Therefore, it is important that we learn to think in the right way and that we understand the creative usefulness of the power of thought.

Particularly when we are erecting "a lighted house", a new personality form, during the Cancer month, it is important to ask ourselves, "What am I really and what has become of me through the environment, upbringing, origin?" In this way one comes ever closer to the perception of one's own inner structure of Being. Meditation is also a help here. Meditation leads us directly to our inner center of Being bringing us into contact with our spiritual qualities and opportunities, leading us to our real depths where we may find unquenchable sources of spiritual power which can lead and direct us in life and which we can apply in the service of our fellow men.

Thus we begin the meditation.

Cancer Meditation

1. Stage: Preparation

During the meditation we sit with a straight back. We close our eyes, but may open them occasionally if tensions arise. We rest our hands on our thighs and place our feet together. We achieve the greatest relaxation of the body by transferring our inner focus to the middle of our body. We let the upper part of our body turn slightly in a circular motion until we have the sensation of sitting at the focal point, at the Hara.

The breath also has a part to play in the preparation for the meditation. We breathe in and out four times. On exhaling we say "Let go—Relax", then we hold our breath for "Become one", we breathe a "Become new", and on holding the breath "Be yourself". The "Let go" comprises all our worries, anxieties, tensions and agitation. The "Relax" is the trusting of ourselves to the fundamental healing powers within. In the "Become one" we surrender ourselves to the real, the original, the Self. In the "Become new" new powers flow into us, and in the "Be yourself" we concentrate these powers within our Ego. We do this a few times.

2. Stage: Alignment

Alignment of the threefold personality, physical, emotional and mental with the Soul. For this exercise in integration we use after every stage the Sacred Word OM in order to shut out all disruptive vibrations.

a) The physical body
I am quite relaxed and am aware of my body. I am sitting on the chair, the chair is borne by the house, the house by the Earth, the Earth by our planetary system. This hierarchy of support secures my existence. I surrender my physical body to heightened perception and consciousness.

OM

b) The emotional body
I have feelings which are connected with desires, desires for love, understanding, security. The emotional world is in continuous movement, changing in color and form with every change of mood. The feelings are calmed by imagining the quiet waters of a lake in which the Sun or the Moon is reflected. I dedicate my emotional body to the transmission of the energies of Love.

OM

c) The mental body
I raise my consciousness to my head, to the center of the brain. I am aware of everything, all impressions are registered, evaluated or ordered. I am wide awake. I see thoughts flowing through my brain; they come from all directions; they penetrate me, an unbroken stream of thoughts. Yet, I myself remain free at the center and observe them, looking at them as if they were children at play.

I, the focus of the consciousness, the I AM on the mental plane, am able to direct my thoughts through my own Will. I have the free choice of only thinking that which is good for me and for all Men. I dedicate my positive, constructive thoughts to the alert recognition of the Good.

OM

3. Stage: Cancer Visualization Exercise

Now I let the focal point of my consciousness glide slowly down from within my head—between my jaws—through my neck—to the upper breast. Here I let it rest. Slowly my attention, my focal point glides down further into my lower body. Here the focal point of my body is also situated, at which I find calmness and relaxation. I let myself sink even further, as into the shaft of a well, until I have penetrated to the source of my Being, to the womb, to the primal source. Here I feel myself to be secure, supported, protected. I can feel the pulse beat of life, I am one with the basis of all life. A deep peace enters me.

I slowly raise myself again, growing out of the womb, becoming bigger, but preserving firmly in my consciousness the connection with the source, with the eternally gushing water of life. I can see a light, like a golden thread of light, shining up from my depths, from the base of my spine, and slowly rising with a fine tone up my spine. First of all from the small of my back, along the spine, quite slowly upwards between the shoulder blades, into the base of the neck and along the back of my neck, over the scalp. I pull the thread of light over my forehead to the base of my nose. There I concentrate on the center between the eyebrows.

Here in the Ajna-center dwells the Ego, the point where the threefold integrated personality converges, the reflexion of the higher Self with which I become one. Then we meditate on the Seed Thought of the sign Cancer.

I build a lighted house and therein dwell.

4. Stage: Group Endeavor

We continue to concentrate on the center between the eyebrows. It begins to grow light, first a small white point, then two leaves of a blue-white lotus flower open. The light shines out over my forehead on both sides flowing slowly out through my temples, becoming ever larger and surrounding in the form of a shining white aura my whole body.

Slowly the white light spreads touching the light of the others, merging with the aura of light of the group. A large white field of light arises which encloses the whole group.

Slowly it begins to turn, becoming ever bigger and spreading upwards in the form of a spiral. A path of light develops which reaches far up into heaven to that source where the Love of God dwells, which is expressed on our planet through Christ.

At the heart of all Love I stand,
From that centre, I the Soul will outward move;
From that centre, I the one who serves will work.
May the love of the devine Self be shed abroad in my heart,
through my group and throughout the world.

In the highest inner concentration we receive the cosmic energies of the sign Cancer and carry them together down the path of light. Then we join with all those who approach the Cancer energies in meditation, dedicating the group to the great process of transmission to humanity.

5. Stage: Transmission To Humanity

We turn to humanity, allowing this living stream of the energy of Light, Love and creative Will to flow through us into the consciousness of Mankind and to spread itself. In so doing we imagine how these powers radiate from numberless points of light and from a net of light spread out over our planet penetrating all areas of our planetary life so that these spiritual powers can effect the events of the world, everywhere and at all times.

We transfer the stream of energy together to humanity through the Great Invocation.

From the point of Light . . .
(see page 234)

OM OM OM

Completion Of The Meditation

We open our eyes inhaling and exhaling once deeply. We move our head, our neck, our shoulders, our feet, our hands. Then we extend to each other our hands, look into each other's eyes and bow before each other.

LEO

Notes • From the collective to individual consciousness •
The element fire •
Ego-testing • True Self-Consciousness • The planetary ruler •
Stages and experiences of Self-Becoming •
The heart of the Leo—the experience of love •
The esoteric seed-thought of Leo •
What actually is the heart? • Polarity: Leo-Aquarius—
Axis of Relationship •
The light of the soul • Leo-Meditation •

LEO

LEO

Notes

Leo	5th sign of the Zodiac
Month	23 July–22 August
Cross	Fixed
Temperament	Fire
Full Moon	Sun in Leo Moon in Aquarius
Houses	5th House/11th House Axis of Relationship
Problem Area	Individual Consciousness— Group Consciousness
Seed Thought	"I am That and That am I."

From The Collective To Individual Consciousness

In Cancer, the deepest point of the Zodiac, we have concerned ourselves with our origin, with our membership of the Collective, of the family and of the source of life. In Leo, we perceive ourselves for the first time to be something individual and distinguishable from others. Mass or Collective Consciousness in Cancer develops to individual consciousness in Leo.

Leo is a Fire sign, and all Fire signs are concerned with the transformation and unfoldment of the Ego. In Leo the individual frees himself from his protecting, defining, but at the same time undifferentiated membership of the Collective and becomes a self-sufficient individual Being. He becomes increasingly aware of his identity or Ego-hood striving for opportunities of individual expression. He creates his own place to live, goes out into the world looking for experiences. He learns increasingly to improve the presentation and realization of his own Ego.

The Leo is the focal point of the world which he has created for himself; the world revolves around him, and he functions as a controlling and acting unity leading and directing others through his personal radiation. He feels himself to be alone in this isolated attitude and thus develops the inner power and strength of a self-enclosed, integrated entity. "The strong alone is the mightiest" is his watchword.

This attitude develops further leading at first to a markedly egocentric consciousness; the Leo ambitiously demands power and influence, prestige, rank and position until such time as he feels himself to be isolated and excluded from the stream of life on his lonely height. Here the inner conversion begins. He longs so intensely for contact, love and understanding that he tears down the walls which he himself has erected between himself and his fellow men. The focus of his consciousness is turned more and more towards his fellow men, towards the group until he no longer feels himself to be an isolated entity standing at the focal point but as a part of the Great Whole. He comes under the group-conscious influence of the opposite sign Aquarius. Responsibility, understanding and sensitivity lead to that self-consciousness which includes everything because it knows itself to be one with everything. This is in short the goal which the Leo should reach through the transforming powers of his own Self.

The Element Fire

In the fire sign Leo the Fire element is concerned in a mysterious way with the inner Self. According to Indian philosophy it is "Fohat", the divine spark in the heart of everyone, which spurs on the development to a self-conscious human being and which drives dynamically in the sign Leo, as in every Fire sign, towards unfoldment.

This fire of consciousness flows through all three Fire signs; in Aries it is concerned with Ego-building, in Leo with self-experience and in Sagittarius with the unfoldment of individual consciousness. Each of these Fire qualities has an effect on self-becoming, purifying or changing the consciousness until it becomes the bearer of the true inner Self bringing the three creative aspects of personality to expression: the spirit in Aries, the Soul in Leo, the body in Sagittarius. In Aries it is cosmic, in Sagittarius planetary and in Leo solar Fire. That is the scientific basis for the unfoldment of the Self in Man to the point where he attains a perfect reflection of the three kinds of divine expression of Being in these three worlds.

Ego-Testing

The Leo must learn to know himself by developing genuine self-awareness. Only then will he know his true Self and his fellow men, too. Therefore, he must first of all free himself from the Collective and test his Ego in the world. This is an adventurous process and leads him into entanglements and frictions with his environment, but also to high flights of Ego-sensation. In this respect he experiences himself as the motivating and originating Ego around which everything else moves. This leads at times either to demands on his fellow men, based on overestimated self-importance, that they must pay attention to him and hold him in esteem, or also to feelings of discouragement and self-contempt.

In Leo we must first of all find out what self-consciousness actually is. Many people are convinced that they are self-conscious whereas they are really only ruled by desires, believing with complete conviction that they have a right to expect their desires to be respected and fulfilled.

True Self-Consciousness

Real self-consciousness however shows itself when a person becomes conscious of his inner power, of his own creative potential recognizing the meaning and purpose of his life and that he has a self-appointed aim in life, a developed and definite program. For this reason it is essential to constantly test oneself to see whether one is only living for oneself or for others as well, whether one is concerned about others turning to one and letting them share a part of one's own inner strength.

Connected with this developed self-consciousness are intelligence, mental perception and a certain amount of integration. If someone is only driven on by emotions and egoistic desires, this is no sign of genuine self-consciousness. If however the Leo is fed and motivated by his central inner Being, then he will radiate genuine, benevolent joy of life from himself, above all in an environment where he is needed and in which his strength and assistance is required and valued.

The Planetary Ruler ☉

The Sun rules in Leo on all three planes: the physical, the emotional and the mental. True, genuine Leos are bearers and givers of light. They irradiate their environment with the warmth of their hearts. The Sun, as the Ruler of this sign, is the power which works from within them out to the world. In this way they have special knowledge about what is central and important in life. This is expressed in the well-known reserve of the Leo, through a concentration of inner powers, so that they can be applied to the full at the right moment. It is surprising what they can accomplish when from these concentrated reserves they dedicate themselves to a goal. Thanks to integrated and purposeful will-power they attain their goal and create advantages for themselves in life because they are always ready to act in decisive situations. They do not allow themselves to be distracted by subsidiary matters but concentrate all their powers on the center, on the goal; they shoot in the dark, but only when they are certain of attaining their goal.

Stages And Experiences Of Self-Becoming

But before the Leo has reached this point he will have to go through various processes of self-becoming. Therefore, we find many variations, many stages. One of these is that he only behaves as if he had already attained genuine self-consciousness. He identifies himself with roles and masks by which he wishes to impress others. If however he identifies too strongly with his role play, with his outer impressive mannerisms, then he will constantly find himself in a difficult conflict with his own feeling of self-estimation, for what he is presenting does not correspond to his self-ideal. Indeed if his pride gets the upper hand, he will then do everything to maintain this illusory Ego. He deceives himself and others and attempts to save his face with all his power. He is then convinced that he must present to himself and others a definite image of himself—a mere outer form, yet behind which he himself is no longer present. His behavior is no longer directed towards the central nucleus of Being but merely towards the requirements of the existing situation and towards the expectations of his fellow men. He behaves completely differently to what he really is. The consequence of this is not only false behavior but also increasing anxiety and feelings of guilt. He tries to be what he is not, estranging himself more and more from his true Self.

There is a special danger here, for it can happen that the Leo no longer finds his way back to himself out of the role which he has been forced to play for such a long time, and so everything that he does and what he achieves through his abilities and talents appears false and distorted for as long as the connection with the original values of his own inner Being is missing. Sooner or later such a development will lead to shipwreck. Nothing is therefore more important for every Leo than to always decide clearly what he really is deep inside himself and what he has made out of himself due to the demands of the outside world: "Where does my adjustment begin; where does the role begin which I must play for the sake of my goal; and what do I myself want?"

It is difficult to recognize such disguises and to dismantle such illusory Egos. Many people use up a large part of their spiritual energy in maintaining their role images at all costs, for they are worried that someone will look within them and be able to recognize the truth.

We all know this anxiety of opening ourselves when we are not certain whether others understand us or simply do not want to hurt us. These protective coverings were usually formed in earliest youth. The infant Ego needs protection and help from without and from within so that the world cannot have a too intensive effect. For our own protection we therefore build certain defensive mechanisms. This was necessary at that time, but it is fateful if as adults we let these protective coverings harden to an impenetrable barrier, simply because we believe that we must hide securely behind them. If we can no longer find our way out of this prison, then we sit lonely behind its walls. It hardly makes sense to live in an empty fortress guarding a false self-image. That is a form of self-deceit which usually arises from the refusal to get to grips with genuine life and to experience oneself. In the end we can only see and hear what serves our self-confirmation and self-love, thus missing opportunities for our own development.

The Heart Of The Leo—The Experience Of Love

The sign Leo is well suited to taking on the venture of his own self-experience and of bursting restrictive barriers with the inner solar power of the heart. In the meeting with others, in the group or in a genuine love affair he can experience his true Self as well as profound inner transformations through love. The heart is indeed ruled by the sign Leo, and it is the heart center which must be developed. Through the awakening of true and genuine love the Leo becomes capable of human relationships which do not strive for the possession, control or sexual use of the other, but is both giving and taking at the same time, similar to the pulse beat of the heart. Far more than in vain self-admiration or anxious encapsulation within himself he is able to clearly recognize in his reaction to others and in the genuine experience of love what he is really like. Thus, he must take on the venture of love without which no transformation and no genuine self-experience is possible.

It is therefore the most important task of the Leo to develop the ability of his own heart for sensitive reaction and to cultivate genuine love. In this way the Leo who is standing at the focal point of his own little universe will become sensitive to impulses from without, to the needs of others to whom he turns his heart and opens his consciousness.

Just as the symbol of the Sun has a dot in the middle and a circle enclosing this focal point, so self-consciousness or the Ego must similarly be prepared to radiate from its focal point out into its environment continuously extending its radius.

The Esoteric Seed Thought Of Leo Runs:

I am That and That am I!

The Leo is therefore two things: inner nucleus and environment. Through the conscious experience of his own Self the Leo develops that spiritual sensitivity which enables him also to recognize and touch the Self in others. In the whole universe it is the awareness and the capacity for sensitivity of the Soul or the power of love, the agent lying at the basis of the Plan of creation, which keeps this development in movement. True self-consciousness is the goal of the whole of human evolution; therefore, the Sun is both exoteric as well as esoteric Ruler of the sign Leo.

If the Leo has his heart in the right place, as it is often put, he will hardly be able to shut himself off through false pride, for he is then not only willing to give but also to receive. It is frequently the case that those born under Leo are too proud to give anything or to help in cases of need. They are of the opinion that they can master or provide everything themselves. In such cases the feeling of Self becomes hard; the power of the heart to radiate is extinguished; he only knows himself and no longer anyone else. It is therefore also important for the Leo always to extend his consciousness and feeling to others in the constant rhythm of giving and taking. He must not lose contact with other human beings becoming lonely, sitting alone on his throne.

As has already been mentioned, the Leo must develop his capacity for sensitive feeling, and indeed not only with regard to his own higher Self but also to his fellow men. This refined ability for sensitive feeling must be expanded until he becomes aware of the unity of all Souls in the sense that "All the Sons of Men are one at heart" or as it is expressed in Sanskrit, "Tat wam asi"—"I am That and That am I".

Because Leo rules the heart, we shall today do a heart-meditation so that we may perceive ourselves inwardly to be that which we really are, so that we may open ourselves like a lotus blossom which shines out into the world with its inner light just like a Sun.

What Actually Is The Heart?

The thread of life is anchored in the heart which maintains our life in a constantly pulsating rhythm letting us partake in the cosmic pulse beat of Being. As soon as our heart ceases to beat, we are physically dead.

But we also have a heart in our feeling body which opens itself and glows when love inflames the heart. We experience the greatest joy and the supremest happiness when two hearts unite in love. If however we have to do without love and understanding, then we suffer in our hearts. If we are without love we feel a constant pressure on our breast. If a loved one turns away from us, then we feel deep within a piercing, boring pain. Our heart contracts and closes. Love sickness or a lack of love can even suffocate the heart. If someone cannot give love, we speak of a "stone heart", of an ice-cold heart; If however one gives love, then the heart center glows. Leo is therefore concerned with the experience of love and with the power of love. There is also a connection between the sign Leo and the Leo-ruled Fifth House, "the House of love and the erotic", and another connection through the axis of polarity Leo-Aquarius, the co-operation of head and heart.

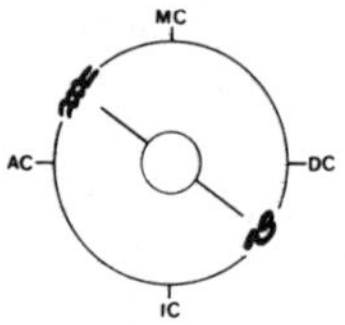

Polarity: Leo-Aquarius
Axis Of Relationship

The correlate on the spiritual plane, or in the mental body, is the relation to Aquarius. This sign, seen from the esoteric point of view, is the reflection in the head of the heart center; here intelligence combines with love and becomes the inner voice, pure reason or wisdom which directs and leads us and which we should without question follow. Many people also call it the "voice of silence" or the Light in the Mind, enlightenment or intuition. Flashes of inspiration really do break into the consciousness of the mind, usually disappearing again quickly. Above all in meditation we continuously experience how a breath of eternity touches us, and we suddenly recognize things which were previously hidden from us. Therefore, we ought to immediately register everything that is seen and touched by means of this spiritual light, even writing it down so that it is not lost. Here rational thought plays a role by indicating, formulating and communicating to the brain what the spiritual Self, the heart or the Soul knows, sees and understands.

When the head and heart are combined, then these intuitions come all the more frequently. Meditation has a special part to play here, for it brings us into contact with our true Self. Thus, the love for all living creatures grows to the same extent as the love for ourselves in the sense of "love thy neighbor as thyself". The wish to serve, to do something for the improvement of conditions becomes stronger. We begin to make ourselves useful, to care with an understanding heart for our fellow men, directing our love to all things that enter our consciousness and extending our own horizons. We interest ourselves more for the problems of the Greater Whole and less for the satisfaction of our own small personal wishes. We engage our intelligence to find solutions to the existing problems of Mankind becoming at last servants of humanity because we know ourselves to be one with all things and recognize ourselves to be a part of the Whole.

That is the development of the person born under Leo once he has combined the polar tension Leo-Aquarius, or head and heart, in his consciousness.

Therefore, we want to concern ourselves today in the meditation, and particularly in the Leo month, with attaining ever greater clarity of consciousness, with being wide awake and highly attentive to the voice of our heart so that Love may shine everywhere and at all times in the heart, as may Light in the mind, illuminating our path and that of our fellow men and giving us a greater insight into the relationship of all things.

The Light Of The Soul

It is the Light of the Soul which gives true self-consciousness and superior sensitivity. That is an important recognition; and thus the connection with the sign Leo becomes clear, the royal sign of the heart, which allows us to become aware of the higher life within ourselves to which we can dedicate ourselves full of confidence and awe. The Light of the Soul grants us the ability to perceive the inner life, becoming and being with all our senses, creating room for it within us and letting it have a free rein—following it.

For this reason it is so very important to listen in to ourselves in meditation and contemplation so that we may be wide awake for directions from deep within us. The most decisive factor here is not necessarily whether a person wants to do good or whether he does bad, but the ability for a superior perception of inner Being. As long as the lustre of the Divine surrounds us and awe and dedication remain alive in our hearts and as long as we subject material goals to our ideals and to our inner values, we are capable of growing further and of developing spiritually. "Only through the magic power of the heart can we reach a higher dimension of consciousness", a Tibetan Master has said.

The superior sensitivity which one can develop to a special extent in the Leo month allows us to see through the form and to penetrate to that inner subjective reality which is hidden from outer objective coverings. This insight into our own life center, which dwells in our hearts, is more than just understanding, sympathy or comprehension. It is the ability to penetrate through all forms and to come to what really is—to life itself which beats in our hearts and unites us with each other.

Thus we begin the meditation.

Leo Meditation

1. Stage: Preparation

During the meditation we sit with a straight back. We close our eyes, but may open them occasionally if tensions arise. We rest our hands on our thighs and place our feet together. We achieve the greatest relaxation of the body by transferring our inner focus to the middle of our body. We let the upper part of our body turn slightly in a circular motion until we have the sensation of sitting at the focal point at the Hara.

The breath also has a part to play in the preparation for the meditation. We breath in and out four times. On exhaling we say, "Let go—Relax", then we hold our breath for "Become one", breath a "Become new ", and on holding the breath "Be yourself". The "Let go" comprises all our worries, anxieties, tensions and agitation. The "Relax" is the trusting of ourselves to the fundamental healing powers within. In the "Become one" we surrender ourselves to the real, the original, the Self. In the "Become new" new powers flow into us, and in the "Be yourself" we concentrate these powers within our Ego. We do this a few times.

2. Stage: Alignment

Alignment of the threefold personality, physical, emotional and mental with the Soul. For this exercise in integration we use after every stage the Sacred Word OM in order to shut out all disruptive vibrations.

a) The physical body
I am quite relaxed and am aware of my body. I am sitting on the chair, the chair is borne by the house, the house by the Earth, the Earth by our planetary system. This hierarchy of support secures my existence. I am quite calm opening my body to the Light of the Soul, dedicating it to heightened perception and consciousness, the perfect expression of the Self.

OM

b) The emotional body
I have feelings of joy, of expectation, but also of insecurity and anxiety. The feeling world varies with every change of mood. I calm it by imagining the calm waters of a lake in which the Moon is reflected.

My emotional body is calm and strong, it is a pure reflector of the Light of the Soul. I dedicate it to the transmission of Divine Love.

OM

c) The mental body

I raise my consciousness to my head, to the center of the brain, to the place where I think. Thoughts come and go, they flow through me. I observe them, like curling waves. I am the observer—I am a center of perceptive calmness. I have the free choice of only thinking that which is good for me and all Men.

I dedicate my thoughts to the creative recognition of the Good.

OM

d) Alignment with the Soul

Now I turn my inner eye upwards, breathe an inaudible OM and join with my Soul, my real Self. From there I can see what I am really like.

3. Stage: Leo Visualization Exercise

I experience myself in my role function. I have many faces; I play different roles. Yet, only a part of me is in my roles, my functions, my duties.

I myself am a center of shining light in my own heart and alert consciousness in my head. I am the true Self and animate my personality, enclosing it within me. I am the Self, the Soul, I expand and radiate Light, Love and understanding like a Sun into my own personality and out to my fellow men.

Thus I am both:

"I am That and That am I"

Then I draw my consciousness up to the highest point in my head, pass quite slowly along the back of my head and down to the base of the neck, fan my consciousness out over my shoulders on both sides and then glide slowly further down my spine. I stop between the shoulder blades feeling a prickling sensation and slip into the ethereal heart center. There I can see with my own eyes a white, closed lotus flower. My face is so close to it that I can smell a fine scent.

I let the OM sound inaudibly, breathing it out onto the closed lotus flower. This slowly begins to open, first of all three outer leaves—the leaves of knowledge, recognition and wisdom.

Then I breathe out once again the sacred word OM, and the three leaves of Love, devotion and inclusion open.

On the third exhalation of the Sacred Word OM, the three innermost leaves open; the leaves of sacrifice, of the joyful Will for creative action and of the co-operation with the Plan of evolution. The scent becomes stronger. At the center of the opened white lotus flower I can see a blue, electric spark to which I surrender myself completely, letting my body be illuminated by it. I become quite still and can feel a pleasant prickling feeling within me.

By forgetting the things which lie behind me, I am completely present within myself listening in extremely attentively to myself until I can hear the voice of my heart by which I joyfully let myself be led

> "At the center of all Love I stand—here nothing can disturb me, here I am one with myself."

4. Stage: Group Endeavor

Then I combine head and heart within me and expand my consciousness out lovingly to all the people here in the room and to all who approach the Full Moon energies in meditation. We are ready to receive the cosmic energies of the sign Leo. We imagine how we all raise a cup together in the highest concentration of inner aspiration and attunement with the spiritual powers of Light and Love which are flowing in to our receptive consciousness—symbolically into the cup.

We slowly raise our hands.

We perceive a path of light which stretches from our group to that source where the Love of God dwells, which is expressed on our planet through Christ. We feel ourselves to be enclosed within His Love and dedicate the group in the great process of transmission to the service of the world.

> "May the love of the divine Self be shed abroad in my heart, through my group and throughout the world."

We slowly lower our hands.

5. Stage: Transmission To Humanity

Then we turn to humanity opening our hearts to our fellow men and letting their needs, worries and burdens flow into us, raising them to the Light of the Soul. From there we pray for help, advice and attention. Then we allow the living stream of the energy of Light, Love and creative Will to flow through us into the consciousness of Mankind and to expand. In so doing we imagine how the powers radiate from numberless points of light, like a net of light spread out over our planet, reaching all areas of our planetary life, so that these spiritual powers can effect the events of the world, everywhere and at all times.

Completion Of The Meditation

We open our eyes inhaling and exhaling once deeply. We move our head, our neck, our shoulders, our feet, our hands. Then we extend to each other our hands, look into each other's eyes and bow before each other.

VIRGO

Notes • The three earth signs: Taurus, Virgo and Capricorn • The difference between Leo and Virgo • Virgo: a sign of service • Polarity: Virgo-Pisces—Axis of Existence • Waiting—maturing—harvesting • Time • Order • Criticism • Expansion—assistance—improvement • Selection—differentiation—confidence in life • The planetary rulers Mercury and the Moon • The three causes of discouragement • Virgo the feminine element • The esoteric seed thought of Virgo • Virgo-Meditation •

VIRGO

VIRGO

Notes

Virgo	6th sign of the Zodiac
Month	23 August–22 September
Cross	Mutable
Temperament	Earth
Full Moon	Sun in Virgo Moon in Pisces
Houses	6th House/12th House Axis of Existence
Problem Area	Opposition of physical and spiritual existence
Seed Thought	"I am the Mother and the Child, I God, I matter am."

The Three Earth Signs: Taurus, Virgo and Capricorn

Today we shall reflect and meditate on the sign qualities of Virgo, an Earth sign on the Mutable Cross. As an Earth sign Virgo is concerned, like Taurus, with the real functions of life. In Taurus the Earth element shows its effect in the maintenance of what exists; everything is done to avoid losses, destruction and the wasting of resources. In Virgo an attempt by all possible means is made to maintain order, to cultivate purity in all things, to care for and look after everything by industrious work. In the third Earth sign Capricorn rules are then made which are to protect life and development within the physical world.

The Difference Between Leo And Virgo

In the last month in the sign Leo a strong self-consciousness was developed. In the Virgo month all overdone Ego-development must be smoothed out and adjusted to reality. The Lion wants to rule, the Virgin to serve. Two opposed elements collide: the positive Leo who wishes to present himself, and the passive, often self-denying Virgo. Through this strong contrast every overemphasis can be smoothed out. If the unification of these two qualities is successful, then creative powers are released which can make good earlier mistakes and heal. For as long as the co-operation of these two forces does not work, a person will vary between overbearing self-confidence and feelings of inferiority, between the will to power and subjection, Ego-establishment and modest reserve, just to name a few of these well-known pairs of opposites.

Seen from a particular point of view, Virgo is supposed to be the oldest of all the signs, previously forming one single sign together with Leo (see "Esoteric Astrology" page 471).

The difference between Leo and Virgo is polar. One of the signs is situated to a certain extent on one side of the see-saw and the other sign on the other side. This expresses itself in life in that the self-assurance of Virgo is frequently made uncertain by Leo (and vice versa, that of Leo through Virgo). The Leo must learn through Virgo that the small things in life are also important, and the Virgo learns through Leo that one should also dare to undertake greater projects. Virgo often doubts that everything is really as simple and correct as Leo thinks. From this uncertainty arises the anxiety that one might do something wrong. It is often this anxiety which reduces the self-confidence of Leo and which frequently drives Virgo to the other extreme.

The latter thinks that only others are doing everything correctly and therefore have a claim to recognition and success. Virgo thinks with bitterness that he is the smallest and lowliest of all, looking humbly up to others who know more than he does, or who behave as if they knew everything and who know how to harness others for their goals with a demonstrative appearance.

Should a Virgo ever try to appear like a Leo, no one would ever take him seriously. It simply does not suit him. His task is to keep the world in order. If nothing great comes of this, feelings of discouragement, meaninglessness or inferiority arise. Here, only the recognition helps that in the great bustle of the world every small cog has its importance and that the whole cannot function without it. If the small details are not correct and there is no one to tend to daily duties, then the great things cannot prosper, either. The Virgoan must spread his spirit out to a greater vision, to an ideal principle of life so that he can work at small things with conviction. It is at all times and in all places the path from the small to the big and vice versa which leads us once again to the center of our own Self.

Virgo: A Sign Of Service

Virgo is a sign of service which concerns itself consciously with the correct use of energies and forms. So today we want to open ourselves for the energies of humility and submission and of our insertion into the Great Whole, of dedication to the innermost life within us and to everything that exists. Thus, loving and dedicated giving to others will develop with the possibility of recognizing the deep needs of others and of knowing how these may be removed. To this end genuine love in purity and inoffensiveness is necessary.

As in all Mutable signs, Love can be easily cultivated in Virgo because it is already present in its basic quality in the Mutable Cross as an essential power. In this respect it is important that the Love is kept free of conditions and demands. It requires self-control, uninterrupted effort, the highest dedication to spiritual ideals to maintain Love even when the troubles of everyday life burden us or when injustice is done to us. Love among Men is not an obvious thing, it must be permitted access and cultivated, requiring daily care. Therefore, it is particularly important during the Virgo month to free ourselves from narrow functional thinking and to grow into the expanse of unpremeditated dedication by opening ourselves entirely to something without ordering it in our thoughts, without selecting the desired aspect of it and without subjecting it to considerations of its usefulness, but by perceiving the whole in pure dedication and thus finding ourselves and others in this process. Here, the polar opposite sign Pisces becomes effective.

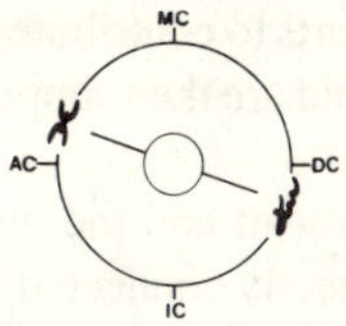

Polarity: Virgo-Pisces
Axis Of Existence

The polarity Virgo-Pisces represents existence in Astrological Psychology. Therefore, Virgo is always struggling for the conquest of existence in a spiritual as well as practical sense. It unceasingly works and creates so that the wheel of life is kept in motion. At the same time however the inner Being, the true Self, must achieve maturity. Here, it is a question of realizing oneself by maturing on the way into our inner Self, not of alienating ourselves. One's task with regard to the world is fulfilled in productive achievement, in work. One's task with regard to the inner Self is fulfilled in human maturity.

What does Man know today of human maturity, when everything is valued according to what he does, what abilities and achievements he can show? When we judge a person, we first of all ask whether he has achieved anything in life, what he is, what position he has or even whether we can rely on him morally, etc. We seldom enquire whether the person in question has a clear mind, whether he possesses inner maturity or whether he is at unity with his own Self.

Virgo demands from us inner maturity and a feeling of responsibility towards the Great Whole so that the small things in life may be done. In this respect there is a danger that these great and profound tasks of Virgo may be overlooked and its qualities hardened and degenerated through limitation. Then this great thread, the deeper sense, may become overlooked and one will remain stuck in the formal or will harden in an infantile condition. It can happen that Virgoans in particular can worry anxiously about their existence. This can be seen in an urge towards material security and delineation. The world becomes a compact, firmly delineated, miniature microcosmos. Whatever does not fit into it, is either misunderstood or rejected. Other people who overstep these limits are energetically criticized.

Waiting—Maturing—Harvesting

In order to understand better the qualities of the sign Virgo, we may observe nature; during the Virgo month of September everything in nature becomes more peaceful. The fiery, expansive forces of Leo have already receded by the end of August, and Man too has become more contemplative. One can sit back for a little, relax and wait until "the fruits of the field have ripened".

The sign Virgo is both the sign of work and service as well as of maturing and harvesting. Through our work, through our personal application we have earned something which we may now receive. Through our co-operation and our energetic efforts to contribute a part to the Great Whole we fit ourselves into the community and are then supported and maintained by the regulating laws of communal life.

The ability to wait and the willingness to mature are spiritual qualities of Virgo and are directly connected with inner Being. In nature the corn ripens in July and is harvested in August–September; in the same way the inner Being grows and ripens according to the natural laws of development. Therefore, life cycles and the time dimension should always be taken into consideration—those iron cosmic laws in accordance with which every process of development unfolds. The Virgoan must not squander his powers; he must learn to wait patiently until the time is ripe.

This becomes clear in the parable of the wise and the stupid maidens; whilst the latter had wasted the oil in their lamps, the others had preserved theirs carefully in order to be able to use it on the arrival of their lord. So we too should not be impatient, losing our faith in life. We should far rather know that in all of us Divine Love, the life of Christ, is deeply rooted and in maturing slowly.

Virgo is concerned with inner development and growth. It will do everything to guarantee security so that nothing damaging or dangerous can penetrate through. This can be clearly seen in the symbol of Virgo with its three closed arches which conceal and protect the inner Being.

Those born under Virgo cannot let their hands rest until they are sure that everything is in order, that they have done everything that must be done. Only when they are convinced that they have done their duty, accomplished their work and contributed their share for the improvement of conditions in the world, can they wait in peace, harvest and enjoy the fruits and receive the wage they have earned.

The ability to wait is a virtue of Virgo, but resignation can result from this very waiting when over a long period of time nothing happens and the fruits fail to appear. Then the Virgoan can lapse into deep disillusionment because he believes all his troubles, cares and work have been pointless. This crisis of pointlessness must always be suffered through; it is best overcome by the knowledge that not only those born under Virgo but all human beings and all living processes have their periods of ebb and flow. In the life of every individual there are times when vision is obscured, the stars concealed and when a dark valley must be travelled through. But once the valley has been traversed, everything goes upwards. Vision follows darkness and the day night. This trust in the conformity of life must be so strong that it assists in overcoming the darkest periods. If the Virgoan lets himself be blinded by the "illusion of the journey through the valley", then he will sink into hopelessness and depression.

The right attitude to life, the right philosophy, religion and the knowledge that others are in greater need are for Virgoans in particular the best method of hauling themselves by "the collar out of the mire", out of discouragement, pointlessness or doubt. They therefore always need a greater vision, an ideal image of themselves and of the world and in addition the certainty that they are needed. Moreover, the hope and the faith that everything has a good end strengthen their Will to life.

Time

The sign Virgo is connected in a mysterious way with time. The ability to wait presupposes confidence in the conformity of life, that everything will take place at the right time. We can transfer this attitude directly into our lives by developing the ability "of having enough time" for the development of human, inner qualities which at the moment perhaps seem unimportant and which serve no direct use or purpose of existence.

Many people are busy from morning until night with senseless fuss loading themselves with work which is of no use to anyone. Such people never have time for the inner life because they take the external too seriously. The perception of the inner man is not a question of having enough time, but of inner time.

Even when we are meditating we must allow ourselves enough time for it. We must do this completely consciously and with conviction, for it is important enough. We must now feel ourselves to be quite free of the worries and duties of others. Afterwards we can be there to serve them all the more deeply, fulfillingly and effectively. During meditation we must and ought to let the feeling arise that we do not have to do anything, that we have dispensed of everything. Above all in the Virgo meditation we must not let ourselves be pushed. Nothing has to be accomplished. We are free. From this attitude and from the feeling of having enough time the inner spiritual qualities spring to the surface by themselves.

Order

Another aspect of Virgo is the love of order. It is always striving to maintain order or to re-establish it. During the Virgo month we all have the opportunity of taking up again something we have let alone or neglected or of completing some work. We can also improve what already exists, removing deficiencies in ourselves and in our environment; we can put right mistakes, make up for something we have left undone in our relations to others, achieving peaceful reconciliation. Virgo is always busy with these matters. It always has in mind the removal of its own deficiencies and those of others, the filling of gaps in education. It is well known that Virgo will always find something more to be criticized in almost everything, something to be improved, to be polished, to be made still more perfect.

Criticism

If the Virgoan, in order to discover his abilities, mistakes and weaknesses, directs himself to his immediate environment, he can become very unpleasant, not only in his criticism but also in his mania for carping. He will find something to complain about in everything; he is satisfied with nothing. A pessimistic attitude to life denying life itself and its possible perfection may develop from this. Through excessive criticism he can also easily damage the beautiful and the valuable in a person seeing only the negative side, the mistakes.

The eye of the Virgoan falls only too easily on the undesireable, the erroneous, the imperfect; he cannot let things go until he has corrected everything. Due to this urge he must bring a thing to order again, whatever it may cost. He must make everything that has been damaged whole or clean again. The law that dwells within him demands it. At the present time this is one of the most important qualities which can make our world whole again. We have so disfigured it that it requires all our powers to save it and to put it in order. We only need to think of environmental pollution, of grievances, illnesses and the wastage of energy. The urge to balance things again, to re-establish order and to put mistakes right are the finest Virgo qualities which radiate into the whole of humanity during this month awakening the hope that everything will be well once again.

But here as well there is a danger that "virtue will become a vice" if we can only see the erroneous, the evil and the ugly. Then we shall become incapable of action and subject to the resignation which grows out of the apparent superiority of evil, making us blind to the recognition that we must begin with ourselves, with the detail which appears so small. We should first of all be satisfied with small things. Also of assistance is a hopeful view of the good in all living things, in the whole of creation, as well as the recognition that there are not only grievances, that all human beings are on the path of development and everyone is basically striving for the conquest of need, errors, illnesses and weaknesses and longing for a better world.

Expansion—Assistance—Improvement

Therefore, the Virgoan should expand his spirit; he should free himself from the small and futile, from his personal, firmly delineated personal sphere and engage himself for the realization of higher ideals. This will assist him in not losing himself in the formal and the insignificant, but rather in engaging his abilities for the blessing of others and for the benefit of the whole. Whether this be as a social worker who uncovers grievances and assists in eradicating them or as a healer who concerns himself with others and recognizes the extent of their cares. Such a person is tirelessly and unceasingly in search of new and better opportunities of solving existing problems so that better living conditions may be created for all. The Virgoans capacity for self-sacrifice is great and their willingness to assist sincere when it is a matter of freeing someone from a position of need.

We too can also revive and cultivate this desire to help and to serve during the Virgo month. Every one of us knows someone whom he can help in some way; to whom he can give his attention and benevolence and who can be freed in this very way from an inner situation of need. As if often the case, a person does not need material help but a certain amount of attention and interest in his problems, an understanding, sympathetic word or piece of helpful advice.

There is also much to be changed in our own character, to be filed down and to be improved. Virgoans work incessantly on themselves in order to perfect their ability for mastering life through learning and further education. They know that they must master something in order to find a place in life and to be able to fight for their existence. Therefore, Virgoans are always concerned to further their knowledge and to evaluate it in practice.

Selection—Differentiation—Confidence In Life

However, they can also so overburden themself with detailed knowledge that they can no longer recognize the overall picture. Therefore, the ability to make the right choice, the selection, is a particularly important ability for a Virgoan to develop. To select what is correct from everything on offer is a first prerequisite for a successful formation of one's life.

The differentiation between the unimportant and the important, between the valuable and the valueless, between quality and quantity, between the real and the unreal brings us into contact with the innermost laws of life. When Virgoans are able to differentiate correctly, they act and live in the confidence in a superior power and in an order of life which forms the basis of all things. Due to this profound conviction they can obey the innermost law of service which is peculiar to Virgo. They will conquer their anxiety about life and about the struggle for existence. Confidence in life must therefore be cultivated so that a greater fulfillment of life becomes possible. This comes about through the talent for differentiation, the analytical capacity of Virgo, who knows what is good for himself and others, and what is harmful.

The Planetary Rulers Mercury And The Moon ☿ ☾

This analytical capacity is associated with the exoteric Ruler Mercury. The esoteric ruler of the sign Virgo is the Moon. As is well known, the latter represents the child or the infant feeling-Ego which wants to be protected and guarded. For this reason, Virgoans lean only too willingly on stronger individuals or on authorities; they prefer to follow the directions and orders of others. When they are discouraged by the excess of tasks to be done, they need someone who can inspire them again with courage and confidence. Discouragement and self-depreciation are two frequent phenomena among those born under Virgo, therefore one must continuously praise them for their work.

The Three Causes Of Discouragement

It is important at this point to clarify the three essential causes of discouragement because not only Virgo, but all of us can be affected by it.

The first cause is frequently a weakening of the life force, an over-exertion of the physical body on account of an excess of duties and tasks. If this is the case, then calmness and relaxation must be cultivated. This is a question of a healthy human understanding. Here the realization is of help that the work of each individual must be adapted to his ability to perform and not to overwhelming necessity.

The second cause is of a more emotional kind. It is the fear of failure when something is required to be done. It lies in the fear of being criticized because one is aware of one's limitations and insufficiencies. Psychologically, this fear is rooted in the fact that one takes one's work too seriously believing that the progress of the world is dependent on the efforts of one individual.

In order to achieve a balance, more humor should be cultivated. One should not take oneself so seriously and under certain circumstances manage to laugh about oneself and one's own weaknesses and limitations. Thus, one will have made a first step towards liberation from a rigid Ego-attitude.

The third cause lies in our mental structure, that is, in the mind. It rests on the capacity to see all sides of a thing. One knows in advance how things could develop and would rather do nothing than expose oneself to any dangers or make a fool of oneself. There is a lack of courage in one's own convictions. One believes that all activity is of no use at all. Thus, one misses out on one's own development and frequently lets pass an opportunity of freeing others from a situation of need. Here the sense for correct proportions must be cultivated. The cure lies in the recognition that it is better to do something instead of remaining inactive, even if activity cannot bring a great success. One must simply be satisfied with small successes in the knowledge that time, eternity and evolution will in the end accomplish all things, and that the whole of creation was not made in one day. The correct feeling for time is decisive here.

Virgo—The Feminine Element

Considered in another way, Virgo is associated with the feminine element in creation. This is a particularly topical theme in the present day, for women are wrestling to obtain the position in society which is due to them, wishing to free themselves from the past. This too comes about through correct differentiation and self-recognition, and leads to a balancing development and to a harmonizing of opposites.

According to Alice A. Bailey, three feminine figures are decisive for the sign Virgo: Eve, Isis and Maria. They are of very special significance for our civilization, for they incorporate symbolically within themselves the whole form nature which, when it is integrated and effective as an organized unity, we call the personality.

Eve is the symbol of the mental nature and human thought, which attains unfoldment through the enticement of knowledge and curiosity. Eve took the apple of recognition from the snake, the material, and in so doing introduced into Mankind the development of the capacity to think. She fell from the unity of consciousness into the duality of good and evil. Since that time Man has been harnessed to this polarity and must—sometimes through painful experience—learn to understand how to differentiate between pairs of opposites.

Isis represents the same on the emotional or feeling plane. In the old Zodiac she was considered to be the symbol of fertility, of motherhood and as the guardian of children. Eve, a symbolic figure, has no child in her arms. The germ is still too small for it to make itself noticeable at this stage. But in Isis the germ sinks down into the desire nature. The mid point between the pairs of opposites has been reached by development being driven on and accelerated through the longing of the desire nature. The vail of illusions and deceits which for so long held us captive on the feeling plane is at last torn apart by clear vision, the recognition of reality. In other words, through Christ-consciousness or through the Light of the Soul. In the "Secret Doctrine" of Blavatsky this process is called "Isis unveiled".

Maria brings the process down to the physical plane at last, to the place of the incarnation bringing the Christ Child into the world there.

In these three Virgins and Mothers of Christ we see the history of human development, those three aspects of personality, physical, emotional, and mental, through which Christ must find expression. The sign Virgo itself indicates a synthesis of these three aspects: Eve thought, Isis feeling, Maria the body.

The Esoteric Seed Thought of Virgo:

I am the Mother and the Child, I God, I matter am.

Looked at from an esoteric point of view, Virgo is also the Cosmic Mother; it is the receptive part with respect to the father-aspect or the positive spirit, and is fertilized by the latter. This truth is preserved for us in the words, "the Holy Ghost overshadowed the Virgin Mary".

In this respect Virgo also represents the "womb of time" in which God's plan slowly comes to maturity and from which with pain and sorrow, through struggle and conflict Christ consciousness is born in the heart. In accordance with the nine months of pregnancy, the true Self grows and matures, the Christ in our heart. Therefore, Virgo is also the sign of profound experience, the place of slow, gentle and yet powerful crises and periodic developments which occur in the dark and yet which lead to the Light.

In accordance with the Seed Thought of the sign, Virgo is at one and the same time mother and child, spirit and matter. The Virgoan should unite both within himself; he should not remain in an infantile, immature state, but should grow into the role of the mother preparing matter for the revelation of the divine Spirit. Thus, Virgo is a sign of service, always busy with, and indeed capable of, maintaining order in the world of form and protecting others from mistakes and mishap.

From an esoteric point of view the sign Virgo has the task of guarding, sustaining and finally revealing the arcane, spiritual reality. The mother guards the germ of the Christ life; matter watches over, sustains and protects the hidden Soul until such time as it manifests itself when its time has come.

The drive to preserve life and the urge to conquer existence are basic motifs of humanity and correspond to the law of matter, to the mother-aspect. The need to love one's fellow men and to understand them is similarly a fundamental impulse of the human Soul or of Christ-consciousness and corresponds to the son- or child-aspect. The urge to serve and to create better conditions in the world for all Men corresponds to the Divine Plan, to the Will or father-aspect. All three together operate through the sign Virgo. Therefore, the service of Mankind is the most effective method for the person born under Virgo of co-operating with his innermost powers of Being and with the laws of life and of making the birth of the true Self possible.

Thus we begin the meditation.

Virgo Meditation

1. Stage: Preparation

During the meditation we sit with a straight back. We close our eyes, but may open them occasionally if tensions arise. We rest our hands on our thighs and place our feet together. We achieve the greatest relaxation of the body by transferring our inner focus to the middle of our body. We let the upper part of our body turn slightly in a circular motion until we have the sensation of sitting at the focal point, at the Hara.

The breath also has a part to play in the preparation for the meditation. We breathe in and out four times. On exhaling we say, "Let go—Relax", then we hold our breath and think "Become one", on inhaling "Become new", we hold our breath, "Be yourself". We do this a few times.

2. Stage: Alignment

Alignment of the threefold personality, physical, emotional and mental with the Soul. For this exercise in integration we use after every stage the Sacred Word OM in order to shut out all disruptive vibrations.

a) The physical body
I am quite relaxed, my body is resting quietly on the chair. I am borne by the chair, I feel secure in this room. I dedicate my body to heightened perception and consciousness.

OM

b) The emotional body
I calm my feelings by imagining a sheet of calm blue water, a lake in which the Sun or Moon is reflected. I dedicate my emotional body to the transmission of Love.

OM

c) The mental body
Thoughts come and go. I remain quite calm listening into myself, looking at my thoughts, I do not let myself be distracted. I dedicate my positive, edifying thoughts to the recognition of everything that is good for me and for humanity.

OM

Alignment with the Soul
We are inwardly secure, attuned to the good and the beautiful, quite prepared to come into contact with our innermost Being.

OM

3. Stage: Virgo Visualization Exercise

I collect my attention into my head, to the place which I exercise when thinking, the brain. I allow the focus of my consciousness to sink down quite slowly within my head, between my jaws, through the neck, until it reaches the upper breast. Here I rest for a moment. Then I slowly descend deeper, down to the stomach region and on further into the center of the body, into the Hara. Here I relax with my whole being.

Then I let the OM sound inaudibly within me, and like waves the sound carries everything with it outwards to the periphery of consciousness: thoughts, desires, worries. Then within me a point of the deepest peace arises, a vacuum, an area empty of air, which surrounds me like a bell of glass. I am in a quiet area of time which envelops me motionlessly and in which I rest.

I have time, an infinite amount of time; nothing is urging me on. The peace and quiet increase, become deeper, tangibly present within me; peace spreads itself, peacefully and deeply. Time stands still; I surrender myself completely to this soundless silence which connects me to infinity. I listen expectantly with all my senses to myself, paying attention to what makes itself heard within me and wants to grow.

Suddenly at the central point of the soundless silence a fine distant tone sounds and at the same time a white point of light appears, like a white shining star in the black firmament. It approaches me becoming larger. The tone too becomes more clearly perceptible until it rises to a crescendo and the light and the tone penetrate my whole body; all the cells of our body vibrate and the light combines over the limits of my body with the light in the whole room around me.

I am the Mother and the Child, I God, I matter.

4. Stage: Group Endeavor

Then we again raise our consciousness into our head and spread it lovingly out to the people in the room. We join with all those who approach the spiritual energies at the Full Moon in meditation. We are as a group unity on the mental plane receptive to the cosmic energies of the sign Virgo.

We imagine how we all raise together a cup into the air in highly concentrated aspiration and attunement with the spiritual powers of Light and Love which flow into our receptive consciousness—symbolically into the cup. We slowly raise our hands.

We perceive a path of light which stretches from our group to that source where the Love of God dwells, which is expressed on our planet by Christ. We feel ourselves to be enclosed within His Love and dedicate the group to the service of the world in the great process of transmission.

At the centre of all love I stand;
From that centre, I the Soul will outward move;
From that centre, I the one who serves will work.
May the love of the devine Self be shed abroad in my heart,
through my group and throughout the world.

We slowly lower our hands.

5. Stage: Transmission To Humanity

Now we turn to humanity letting the needs, worries and burdens of others flow into us, raising them to the Light of the Soul and praying for help from that source.

We allow the living stream of the energy of Light, Love and creative Will to flow out through us. In so doing we imagine how these powers radiate from numberless points of light, like a net of light spread out over our planet, reaching all areas of our planetary life, so that these spiritual powers can effect the events of the world, everywhere and at all times.

Together we transmit the energy stream to humanity through the Great Invocation:

From the point of Light . . .
(see page 234)

OM OM OM

Completion Of The Meditation

We open our eyes, breathe in and out deeply once, moving our head, our neck, our shoulders, our hands and our feet. Then we extend to each other our hands, look into each other's eyes and bow before each other.

LIBRA

Notes • The scales • Peace—harmony—justice •
Crises of decision • Knowledge and wisdom •
The difference: Virgo–Libra •
Justice—equilibrium • The sign of you and of partnership •
The Libran • Polarity: Aris–Libra–Axis of encounter •
The planetary rulers •
Parting of the ways—correct choice—knife-edged path •
The esoteric seed thought of the sign Libra •
Meditation and alignment • Libra-Meditation

LIBRA

LIBRA

Notes

Libra	7th sign of the Zodiac
Month 23	23 September–23 October
Cross	Cardinal
Temperament	Air
Full Moon	Sun in Libra Moon in Aries
Houses	7th House/1st House Axis of Encounter
Problem Area	Opposition of I and YOU Problems with contacts
Planetary Rulers	exoterically Venus esoterically Uranus
Seed Thought	"I choose the way which leads between the two great lines of force."

The Scales

When we think of Libra, the picture of a pair of scales immediately comes into our mind, there are two scales and a little measuring tongue in the middle. This little tongue should always be in the middle. This is achieved when both sides, both scales are in balance. But we also recognize that the slightest deviation destroys the balance; the little tongue will move from one side to the other. Librans react just as sensitively to the fluctuations in their environment. They perceive the mildest unevenness and the slightest indication of disturbing fluctuations, losing their sense of balance easily.

In the present day world we are exposed to so many disturbing factors, whether this be the constant noise, or duties and demands on performance. Man has always had to struggle with incidents, impressions and disturbances. In the end he developed in his mastery of conflicts into that which he is today. The Libran should also learn to manage disturbances and conflicts, even accepting these as meaningful or as an opportunity to develop further.

During the Libra month we can take care that our attitude of rejection towards incidents which disturb our peace and comfort does not increase. Otherwise we should continuously lose our sense of balance. If, on the other hand, we place ourselves in the middle of constantly fluctuating inner and outer circumstances, then we identify with the little tongue on the scales achieving in so doing a dynamic point of balance in our own nucleus of being. From there, that is from our own center, we can react flexibly to the constantly changing situations of life. We are then no longer so susceptible to every disturbance from without, no longer immediately for or against a thing or a person, but able to build a bridge of understanding and agreement between warring forces, thus establishing a balance everywhere.

Peace—Harmony—Justice

Librans have a love of peace which is deeply rooted in their hearts and a strong desire for harmony. However, as such refined and ideal desires can only be realized with difficulty in the raw struggle of life, they are always ready to compromise. This has given the Libra type the reputation of being superficial and soft. They like to avoid hard disagreements and conflicts or the clear defense of an opinion because Libra is the symbol of the agreement, of the weighing and pondering of different points of view. At the same time Libra has a finely developed sense of justice. It can create harmony and agreement where conflict rules; it bridges contrasts within the community.

Crises Of Decision

In his efforts to avoid conflicts and arguments the Libran often falls prey to indecisiveness. He does not wish to cause anyone pain and wants to be just to all, which is of course impossible and carries the additional danger of dissipating the impulse of Will and the objectives of life.

We know Librans who are continuously going through crises of decision. In these cases the fear of stress, possible mistakes or eventual conflicts can become so great that nothing at all is done and decisions are simply left to the future where it would have been better to intervene oneself. To a great extent Librans only act when nothing else is possible or when fate has given the impetus in some way or another. Sometimes they simply challenge others to force them to a decision as they themselves do not know what they want. They must however learn without fail to become capable of making decisions for themselves, of recognizing for themselves what is good and right. This is the spiritual task of the Libran.

As Libra is the sign of balance, everything is carefully evaluated and weighed up in order to grasp the finest nuances and differences in quality. It is not simply a matter of black and white, good and bad, evil and just nor of seeking agreement according to the principle "As you do to me, so I to you". That would only achieve a statistical balance which one would have to correct again and again, just like the weight on a pair of scales which must remain the same on both sides. It is much more a matter of finding a dynamic balance which is achieved through the careful recognition of differences in quality and through a clear capacity for judgement and differentiation as well as through the ability to stand incorruptibly at one's own center. Therefore, it becomes increasingly more difficult on the spiritual path of development to make correct judgements and correct decisions. But this weighing and careful judging lead to the "knife-edged path" which Man must find and travel in the sign Libra. Here is the transition in the Horoscope from the unconscious to the conscious area.

Knowledge And Wisdom

Libra is indeed the first sign above the horizon; here one enters the light of day. Man leaves the learning phase of the lower sins. The path leads from the "hall of knowledge and learning", as one may also call the other, unconscious area, up to the "hall of understanding and wisdom". "Knowledge" refers to everything that can be diagnosed and defined, what can be accepted intellectually as certain fact and verified through experiment. It concerns the material side of the events of development. "Wisdom" refers to higher reason, to the development of life within the ever changing outer coverings and forms and within expanding consciousness. It is the intuitive perception of truth, independent of intellectual judgement and standardized measurements. Wisdom is the ability to adapt oneself more and more to higher measurements. Through the recognition of the universal laws of development and of Universal Love onesided judgements and condemnation can no longer be made. A wise man understands everything because he has an overall view of the events of development. he can see the beginning and the end of a situation. This is made clear in the old wise saying, "the more a man knows, the less he will judge". This development starts with the sign Libra above the horizon.

The Difference: Virgo–Libra

Seen from the esoteric point of view the turning of the wheel takes place in Libra, for here one has to decide to which side the scales are to tip; either to continue on the side of concentration on the material or to spiritual development, either back to Virgo or on to the sign Scorpio. The Virgo life, which is placed below Libra on the wheel (corresponding to the Moon's Nodes-Point), can be the life of a materialistic person under the influence of the material aspects of Virgo, of the mother, or it will gradually show a fluctuation of the Soul indicating the arcane, spiritual life whose predetermined guardian and keeper is the Virgo-mother (as we heard in the last chapter). After the turning of the wheel the path leads on to Scorpio. The active life of the Soul starts with those tests and struggles which must be overcome in Scorpio and which take place predominantly between the personality and the Soul, between lower and higher inclinations, between material and spiritual values.

Libra symbolizes the intermediate stage, the point of balance, between these two conditions. In the forward thrusts of development, in crises of decision the scales fluctuate from left to right and up and down. The Libran swings as it were between these two pairs of opposites. Therefore, this sign is very important for spiritual development, but also very difficult. Here one experiences the curious "see-saw experience" which first of all proves itself to be confusing for a person when on the one hand he attempts to be a complete person enjoying life, while on the other hand feeling at the same time within himself the impulse to strive for higher values. Even if he concentrates totally on the spiritual life, he still feels himself drawn back to old habits and desires.

Justice—Equilibrium

Libra is sometimes called the "place of judgement", for it is here that the decision is made and the die is cast which separate the "sheep from the goats". At the present time we are also drastically experiencing this selection in politics and economics. Since 1969 Pluto has been passing through the sign Libra and since that date it has increasingly occurred on the world stage that anyone who up until then had been sitting securely on his throne, allowing himself all possible machinations, was suddenly unmasked losing his power and dignity. For some years we have also been experiencing the process of equalization within partnerships, within the family and within businesses. Everything is striving towards equilibrium. Even in nature we can observe that Man has now recognized how seriously he has exploited and disfigured nature. The protection of the environment became important, birth control was encouraged; the oil crisis was followed by economic recession. All these phenomena are attempts by nature to re-establish the equilibrium destroyed by the folly of Man.

Thus, this Libra month offers us all an opportunity of clearing up our imbalances. We should observe ourselves and recognize if we are living in some extreme or other. Perhaps we react to a certain matter too sensitively and must become more objective and tolerant. Perhaps we sleep or speak too much, perhaps we eat and drink or smoke excessively; perhaps we have far more of something than we need. Now is a good time to free ourselves of it and to find moderation in all things again. The law of equalizing justice is active. Perhaps we must also make peace with someone or other, forgiving him if he has apparently done us wrong.

There are so many possibilities, not only in material but also in psychological matters, of being out of balance or of being disturbed by other people; without it being any of our doing, we can make enemies; without wishing it, hostility can arise from some objective conflict or other. If we can manage, when standing up for our own interests, to also appreciate the position of the other person and to let him feel that we understand and respect him as a human being, in spite of objectively opposed fronts, then an equalizing, just solution can be found. The sign Libra is exceptionally well suited to working out just agreements and has already produced in a positive sense many a perfect diplomat.

The Sign Of YOU and Of Partnerships

In the horoscope the sign Libra is the YOU-sign. It is situated far-removed in the YOU-area on the righthand side of the horoscope and is therefore concerned to a special extent with contact and human relationships. (You will find more about the division of the horoscope in the book "Man And His World"). Without a You, without a partner Libra cannot really be happy. It is always looking for the right partner, for the genuinely harmonious equilibrium, not only in human relationships, but also in love and marriage.

Those crises of development and decision which are always causing the Libran to lose his balance usually take place in the area of contact. Love can hurl him into the highest happiness, but also into the deepest suffering. He is always struggling in some way or other with love because he longs for a partner who understands him completely, who even bears him in his or her hands freeing from all worries about existence. However, he often evaluates the other person, the partner, according to whether he or she can fulfill his wishes and serve other purposes. So the other is not seen as that which he or she really is, but as how he can be made useful or exploited. In this way, vision is narrowed. The partner cannot be perceived in his or her true being, depth and breadth; true love cannot manifest itself.

The Libran

He must therefore learn that such an attitude causes dependence on the partner and that he cannot develop in such a way. In a good partnership both parties must contribute their share so that a genuine exchange, honest companionship and absolute trust can arise. This frequently demands from the Libran however the renunciation of egoistic demands, understanding and gratitude, justice and the desire to be loved until such time as he himself has become genuinely capable of being loved. All selfish goals with regard to marriage and partnership, all manipulative mechanisms of contact, which the Libra type can use so expertly, must at last be purified in the melting pot of suffering through love.

After such a purification and inner conversion the Libran will become capable of facing people without prejudices and, thanks to a sensitive sense of justice, of giving them what they deserve. He knows when he approaches a person with preconceived intentions or prejudice that he is not aiming at the entirety of his Being but only at a particular part; he does not learn the whole truth about the other and can therefore not make a correct judgement.

In the Libra month we too can learn in our attitude to contacts that for a free and true meeting with a person we must be unpremeditated and selfless by allowing the other the freedom to be himself. Thus we come into contact with the other to the extent of our whole Being; true meeting and communication become possible. The requisites for Love among Men, which at the same time liberate one's own being, are therefore a lack of premeditation and inoffensiveness. A great thinker once said, "It is one of the profoundest paradoxes of life that a Man by thinking less of himself becomes more fully himself". Whoever becomes selfless or unpremeditated grows into his true Being, becoming capable of selfless Love.

As soon as we permit our Self, and thereby also love for all creatures, to work through us on the world, the world around us will also be transformed. If we remain in this condition of love, even maintaining it in times of difficulty, then we shall continuously transform ourselves and will be called to ever newer tasks. Through our own transformation we shall also see the world and human beings in quite another way; many things will be seen in a new light. For the Libran the love streaming out of his own center of Being is the dynamic point of balance which unites all the extremes of life and joins him in harmony with others.

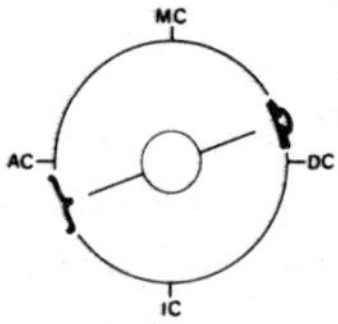

Polarity: Aries–Libra
Axis of Encounter

In the polar tension Aries–Libra the human problem of EGO and YOU shows itself, which often becomes acute in many cases during the Libra month. If, for example, the Libran whose Ego is not yet firm has found a partner, he tends to look for his own Ego in the partner and to live outside his own Self. He will look for stability and security from the other, which he will only find temporarily. Only through disappointments or rejection will he slowly learn to remain himself, even in the greatest love. He must preserve his own point of balance at his own center. He must not lose himself in a loved one, must not hold fast to YOU believing that he cannot live without the other person. He must "release" the YOU from this very love giving him the freedom to be himself. Only in this way can love really blossom.

Once he has become united with himself and behaves correspondingly, once he is so to speak "a perfect whole", has found his own center and can maintain it, then quiet balance, security and superior calmness will enthuse his fellow men with confidence. Only then can he begin with a genuine partnership in which both parties stand side by side complementing each other.

Only a person secure within himself and self-conscious (Aries) also has the opportunity of reacting really genuinely and honestly towards others and of turning to them with complete sympathy (Libra) without in so doing being damaged in his own Selfness. He can even let himself be affected, indeed shaken, by the fate of another without being thus overturned himself. Such a person is free for relationships with others and can work both as an ordering and equalizing factor at the same time. However, whoever has not yet learned to cope with his own imbalance and is correspondingly unsure and restricted within can hardly turn to others freely and openly. Peace, harmony and agreement with oneself are therefore the first prerequisites for good contacts with others and should be particularly cultivated in the Libra month.

The Planetary Rulers ♀ ♅

As harmony with and just love for the YOU are goals worth striving after for the Libran, it is also important to achieve a conscious valuation of things. This occurs through the development of the capacity to differentiate with the help of the planetary Rulers. The traditional Ruler of Libra is Venus; the esoteric Ruler is Uranus.

Venus tries with all her means to maintain the condition of harmony, but also of comfort. She does not wish to exert herself. She always looks for the easiest solution and would like comfort in all things; be this through constant care for beauty and suitability—frequently through outward elegance—or be this through an egoism open to compromise, a "blowing the way the wind blows".

Uranus as the esoteric Ruler of this sign only has an effect when one sets out on the spiritual path. Through higher understanding he leads to a greater capacity to differentiate. The Libran will become capable of weighing things carefully and thus making the right choice between the material and the spiritual values of our existence. In this way he grows into a higher state of consciousness which leads to self-becoming.

Every step towards higher values and towards greater reality demands however the renunciation of something small. One must therefore give up many things, perhaps even favorite things, in order to gain greater ones, in order to be able to grow into giving and mature love. The Libran wants to be loved and admired but must learn that he must first become capable of true love before he can experience the unison of the Souls.

In a certain way meditation also demands renunciation. All external diversions, thoughts, worries and desires must move into the background. Only in this way can we give ourselves entirely to a thing. This demands the rejection of everything superficial and empty which only attracts externally. Yet not only meditation alone can we become free of these things; the struggle for freedom must also be carried on out in the world, manifesting itself in the next month in the great struggle and victory in the sign Scorpio. However meditation can be of assistance to us now in finding the correct orientation and in growing into spiritual valences.

Parting Of The Ways—Correct Choice—Knife-Edged Path

Considered esoterically, Libra is the sign of decision; the Soul stands at the parting of ways and must choose the right way. It is the forking of the path which is connected with the appearance over the horizon. In Libra Man beholds for the first time a vision of the spiritual path and of the individual goal of development. At the Point of Age we pass over the horizon and can look beyond along the horizontal line to the Ego, to the Ascendant, to the orientation of life. Now we are concerned with the correct relationship between EGO and YOU, with genuine humanity and partnership.

A developed Libran may no longer allow himself to act and judge on the basis of false motives. In so doing he would give way to the impulse of his egocentric feeling nature or to the unconscious area of the horoscope. Whether this occurs because of a momentary mood, self-defense or because of thoughts of revenge, is of no importance. These human inclinations should be overcome as well as possible on the way to conscious individualization, on the way upwards to the highest point in the horoscope.

The trials of Libra are as follows:

1. He must not let himself be influenced or corrupted in his judgement of other people.
2. He should not attach himself to the strongest opinion or to the strongest power.
3. When it is a question of the truth about another person, he should under no circumstances give way to personal prejudices or collective forces. Otherwise he is in danger of doing injustice to others who have placed their confidence in him, and will fluctuate between contrasts in the sense, "Today you acclaim him, tomorrow you will cry crucify Him". This attitude would drive him into painful conflicts of conscience and feelings of guilt with periodically occurring depressions. As has already been said, Libra must take the middle way, whereby the correct point of view will be found through objectivity. In the final analysis truth is the little tongue in the middle of the scales.

The Esoteric Seed Thought Of The Sign Libra

I choose the way that leads between the
two great lines of force.

This way is the path which leads between the two pairs of opposites of our existence. That "knife-edged path"—as it is so called—must always be kept in view by the Libran so that things do not go to extremes but remain firmly at the center of our own Self and that he can keep the dynamic point of balance.

As has already been mentioned, this condition is not static but dynamic, as a tight-rope dancer on a high tight-rope struggling for his balance and in so doing always moving forward.

In a YOU-relationship the Libran must recognize that he may neither judge from his own point of view nor go over completely to the point of view of the other. He must take up the middle on the axis of encounter and recognize with distance, detached from personal opinions, where everyone stands and what is correct for each person at that particular moment. From the middle of the way he can grant the YOU, the partner, the right to be himself without dependency, without exaction, freely and honestly. Here he can make correct decisions which not only have an intelligible relation to the inner area of life but which also fulfill the demands the external situation is making at the time.

Such a purified Libran will be asked for wise advice, for he creates agreement in the world and allows justice to all. Nothing will be rejected or accepted as true, but everything will be tested for its correctness. In so doing the Libran's sense of justice as well as his capacity for love are frequently put to a constant hard test, for he may in no way pursue personal goals. The developed Libran is a just judge and is represented symbolically with blindfolded eyes.

Librans must therefore seek the knife-edged path, find it and travel along it, thus liberating themselves from extreme contrasts. That is the meaning of the Seed Thought and the spiritual task of all those born under Libra.

Meditation And Alignment

In meditation in general and today in particular we are concerned with the dynamic point of balance in order to balance out pairs of opposites. This is the fundamental law of alignment per se, the alignment of the threefold personality and above all of the personality with the Soul, with the higher Self.

A Tibetan Master once formulated this very nicely: "The implementation of our personal "tool" and the creation of a vacuum, of an unimpeded line of connection between the physical brain and the higher Self, the Soul, bring about the emission of divine realization".

During this practice in alignment it is a good idea to imagine the human brain as an "inner eye". At the point where the alignment is to take place the inner eye or attention must be turned upwards in an attempt to arrive at a superior plane—like a juggler balancing a ball on his nose. This process can also be compared to the breath.

On inhaling one collects one's powers; one draws breath from the profoundest depths of one's Being. With full lungs the breath is held for a while. During this intermediary stage the alignment takes place in the greatest concentration and one reaches internally the next highest stage. If the breath is held for a longer period of time all the life forces are held firmly at the point of rest, of silence or at the point of balance. When inhaling the inner eye is turned upwards and remains in this upward looking attitude. It lifts so to speak the threefold personality upwards "to the Light of the Soul".

This is not achieved simply by holding the breath and looking attentively upwards with the inner eye. At this stage of the highest concentration of looking, hearing and feeling one must at the same time remain in an attitude of the greatest relaxation within tension. One must so to speak allow oneself to fall back again into the center of one's own Being, yet maintaining the tension, expansion or alignment.

We can imagine this pictorially as an expanding, shining, white sphere which arises around the body. Thanks to our gift of imagination we can experience this with our senses. Once we have reached the radius, we must bring our consciousness back to the center and at the same time hold on to the radius. By bringing the focus of consciousness back from the radius to the center a kind of vacuum or magnetic field arises into which the energies of the Soul can flow.

One can also speak of Libra in the sense of meditation as an "interval between two activities". This explains that stage of meditation which we call contemplation. It is this strange condition just described which is so difficult for us Europeans to understand and which Laotze describes as "acting within inactivity". It is the highest tension with simultaneous relaxation. First of all it is important to find the exact middle between an overemphasizedly positive and a too negative attitude of spirit, between energetic action and inactivity, between spiritual productivity and passive preoccupation.

This can also be represented as listening to a far off sound to which all senses are directed. In so doing we must become completely quiet and peaceful within. Usually we hold our breath; we are far from all external disturbances; every nerve is tensed to receive even the faintest sound. This attentive listening attitude must be combined with a positive watchfulness, thus the correct degree of tension is achieved. Once we have achieved this however, we are not in a position to maintain it for more than a few moments. "One cannot stand on tiptoe for ever", Laotze once wrote.

We cannot only listen to a distant sound with our inner senses, but also fully perceive the YOU, our fellow man, as he really is. We can turn to him with increased sensitivity recognizing his need, but nevertheless remaining ourselves. Today at the Libra Full Moon it is pertinent that we should make a special effort to come to an agreement with the YOU, with our partner, with our fellow man. We allow our heart to be moved by the intense desire to achieve peace, love and harmony with all creatures.

We can strive for this attitude of loving understanding in every dual or polar relationship, whether this be with our friends, colleagues at work, marriage partners or children. Everywhere we can now strive for a genuine agreement. We can even join with our own Soul and establish a relationship of partnership with her by practicing alignment and by opening ourselves to our own innermost Being, allowing it to work through us, becoming one with all those who have already passed along this way before us. Through this experience of unity we recognize that every human being exists for himself alone and yet is a part of the Greater Whole, that the energies which maintain us and all things in life are the energies of the ONE LIFE in which we live, move and have our being.

Thus we begin the meditation.

Libra Meditation

1. Stage: Preparation

During the meditation we sit with a straight back. We close our eyes, but may open them occasionally if tensions arise. We rest our hands on our thighs and place our feet together. We achieve the greatest relaxation of the body by transferring our inner focus to the middle of our body. We let the upper part of our body turn slightly in a circular motion until we have the sensation of sitting at the focal point, at the Hara.

The breath also has a part to play in the preparation for the meditation. We breathe in and out four times. On exhaling we say "Let go—Relax", then we hold our breath and think "Become one", on inhaling "Become new", we hold our breath, "Be yourself". We do this a few times. Then we allow our breath to come and go quite freely and think "We breathe".

2. Stage: Alignment

Alignment of the threefold personality, physical, emotional and mental with the Soul. For this exercise in integration we use after every stage the Sacred Word OM in order to shut out all disruptive vibrations.

a) The Physical Body
I am quite relaxed, my body is resting calmly on the chair, I am borne by the chair, I feel secure in the room. I surrender my physical body to heightened perception and consciousness.

OM

b) The Emotional Body
I calm my feelings by imagining a sheet of calm blue water, a lake in which the Sun or Moon is reflected. My feeling body reflects the Light of the Soul. I dedicate my feeling body to the transmission of Love.

OM

c) The Mental Body

Thoughts come and go. I remain quite calm listening into myself, looking at my thoughts without letting myself be distracted. I dedicate my positive, edifying thoughts to the growing recognition of everything that is good for me and for humanity.

OM

d) Alignment With The Soul

I surrender myself fully to the life of my Soul which flows into me in its full abundance. From the depths of my Being currents of the highest power of consciousness well up and seek form within me. From above cosmis forces of Light flow into me. The two currents of power meet within me. I am like the bed of a river through which the cosmic life current flows. I remain quite still and meditate on the Seed Thought of Libra:

I choose the way that leads between
the two great lines of force

3. Stage: Libra Visualization Exercise

Everything within me is silent listening, sacred silence. I can see a white path of light before me, narrow and straight. At the end I can see a golden-white gate; it is closed. Very slowly I place a foot on the path of light and attempt to hold my balance. Then I slowly push my other foot forward. With my eyes on the gate I balance my way forward along this "knife-edge path". I use my hands to maintain my balance.

A magic force emanates from the gate which draws me, which becomes ever stronger, which envelops me and maintains my balance. Without turning away I hold it in view striding slowly forwards. As I approach nearer the two folding doors open. A shining light breaks out and illuminates the path on which I am now striding ever more confidently forwards. I pass unhindered through the gate into the light. . . .

a) I am now standing looking my own Soul in the face, my true Self. b) I, the personal Self, and the Soul are in essence one single reality. c) In reality there is no division or duality but only a unity, a Son of God in manifestation whose Being is light. I let the OM sound in the silence. Then I bring the life and the Light of the Soul slowly back into my body. I imagine how this light penetrates my body, my whole personality, illuminates my thoughts, making my feeling nature positive and calm and strengthening and animating the physical body.

4. Stage: Group Endeavor

Then I emit thought-currents of Love, power and Light to all who suffer or are searching in the world. I feel one with all life, with all beings. I know that a Spirit bears and maintains all existence, and I affirm:

I am one with my group brothers
and all what I have is theirs.
May the love of my Soul pour forth to them;
May the power which is in me raise and lead them;
May the thoughts, which my soul creates reach
and encourage them.

Like waves an echo of gratefulness and love flows back from them to me, awakening in me joy and happiness which I openly accept.

We create from this loving joy a path of light which stretches from humanity to that source where the Love of God dwells, which is expressed on our planet through Christ. We feel ourselves to be enclosed within His Love and dedicate the group to the service of the world.

5. Stage: Transmission To Humanity

Then we turn to the whole of Mankind. We allow the living stream of the energy of Light, Love and creative Will to flow through us into the consciousness of Mankind and to expand. In so doing we imagine how these powers radiate from numberless points of light and from a net of light spread out over our planet penetrating all areas of our planetary life. We slowly raise our hands and transmit the energy stream in all directions:

Light, Love and power to all beings
in the North–South–East–West, above and below.
Love, joy and peace to all beings

Then we say together the Great Invocation.

From the point of Light . . .
(see page 234)

OM OM OM

Completion Of The Meditation (as before)

SCORPIO

Notes • The difference: Scorpio–Libra •
The process of death and becoming •
Polarity: Taurus–Scorpio—Axis of possession •
The sign ruler Mars • Discord • Conflict between life and death •
The esoteric seed thought of Scorpio •
Spiritual rebirth • Conversion, change, transmutation and victory •
The demolition of the "little Self" •
The threefold tests in the sign Scorpio •
The "Dweller on the Threshold" •
Basic exercise in meditation • Scorpio–Meditation •

SCORPIO

SCORPIO

Notes

Scorpio	8th sign of the Zodiac
Month	24 October–22 November
Cross	Fixed
Temperament	Water
Full Moon	Sun in Scorpio Moon in Taurus
Houses	8th House/2nd House Axis of Possession
Problem Area	Yours and Mine, Taking and Giving
Planetary Rulers	exoterically Mars esoterically Mars
Seed Thought	"Warrior I am, and from the battle I emerge triumphant."

The Difference: Scorpio–Libra

On crossing the horizon we entered the area of consciousness in the horoscope and attained in Libra a point of rest which is destroyed again in Scorpio in order that the development may continue. In Scorpio the inner Being, the consciousness of the Self, forces itself outwards. It finds itself in conflict with the forms which have been created so far. Therefore, Scorpio is a sign of crisis, a sign of conversion, of reorientation, of transformation which begins with the destruction of harmony and of the balance achieved in the sign Libra. The laws of life and of development are at work here effecting the eternal transformations in the world of form.

The changes and uncertainties which arise from this are not easy for the fixed Scorpion to understand if he is determined to hold on to what has been established in the belief that there is here an apparent security. Therefore, one of the most important lessons for a Scorpion to learn is that in development there can never be a standing still, nor any holding on and no absolute security, but that it requires continuous striving forward and a flexible reaction to all transformations which life may bring. Finally, he must find security in insecurity. This condition is called continuous consciousness. Consciousness is only continuous however when it is in constant movement holding fast to nothing, when it is always flowing and journeying.

The Process Of Death And Becoming

In order to keep this movement flowing, the Scorpion must continuously go through processes of death and becoming. He must free himself from material captivity and learn to live with the uncertainties. He is incessantly creating new forms; he clings to these, but will destroy them again immediately because they do not satisfy him and hold him back in his development. Therefore the psychological and spiritual demand for eternal death and becoming lies in Scorpio.

This law of "death and becoming" underlies everything that lives, whether we happen to be born in Scorpio or not. Everywhere, out there in nature as well as in the late Fall, we experience dying, struggling, the stormy wind which tears the leaves from the trees. Whoever resists these laws of life in a hardened or anxious manner will undergo crises in Scorpio and suffer from constant fear of loss.

For the person living in spiritual consciousness however life and death, dying and becoming are in fact one and the same, for he knows that every cyclical development in life is subject to this process. He also knows that all becoming is preceeded by a dying. The old leaves must fall away from the tree so that the new ones can grow. This process contains that power which keeps the process of creation in motion. Goethe also recognized this when he said,

If not by thee possess'd, this death and birth, thou art a mere sad guest on this fine earth.

We too can free ourselves during the Scorpio month from the obstructive chains of the restrictive Ego which clings to material things. Whoever can free himself and make himself receptive to whatever is greater than his narrow circle, greater than his small Ego, he wins the great inner freedom which leads on in the next month to the sign Sagittarius. Without this experience we should move backwards through the Zodiac. It is impossible for a person to mean something to the YOU, to really serve his marriage partner, his family or the community, to achieve something as an artist or educator without being familiar with this process of death and becoming or without learning to cope with the transforming force of Scorpio.

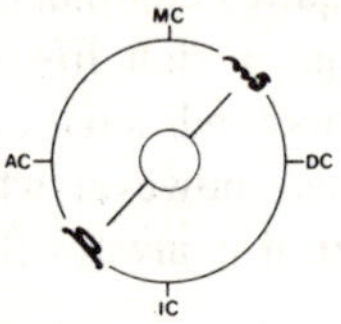

Polarity: Taurus–Scorpio
Axis of Possession

The polarity between Taurus and Scorpio causes us to become conscious of this process of death and becoming. First of all we notice our own limitations, inflexibility, obstinacy and material captivity. The walls and boundaries which the Taurean so easily erects to protect his own Ego, his own possessions and comfort must be breached and torn down in Scorpio so that the way is made free for new-becoming and further development.

These protective walls are made up of all those things which we are used to and which we love. It is the "small Ego" which is worried about its existence, this narrow Being with its inveterate forms of thought, its hardened claims to an undisturbed, comfortable life in security, preserved in an edifice of things known and trusted. It is that "small Ego" which only thinks of itself and of its prosperity, which regards the possessions of others with envy, which can never get enough, always considering how it can get hold of still more, which in conflict situations repays according to the old law of a "tooth for a tooth". This hardened and confining attitude to life, of only worrying about oneself, hinders a person in obtaining pure maturity and development. In the Scorpio month we are all confronted with our own limitations, protective walls and egoisms; we can supersede these by dismantling our false forms of behavior and beginning a new life.

Like everyone else the Scorpion is striving for security, harmony and peace. But he rarely attains what he seeks. Life itself or, to express it better, the power of the own Self, the inner drive to self-actualization destroys egoistic desires and confining limits, knocking down what wants to become established, turning over what seems to be secure, undoing what has been bound, pulling away the floor on which he believes himself to be standing securely.

Therefore, the life of the person born under Scorpio is a constant struggle; he is full of insecurities, doubts and absurdities, full of contradictions and spiritual crises. In inner spiritual development the law of development is at work, of further growth, not of establishment. Movement is meant, not standing still. Scorpio is indeed the "dead point" or "trough" in the Zodiac. As soon as we stand still holding on anxiously to old rights or believing that we may relax, we receive a symbolic "push from behind". Just like the example in the Bible of Lot's wife who looked around and turned into a pillar of salt, so in Scorpio one can similarly fall prey to destructive forces. Instead of becoming transparent for the inner being, which in passing on through the Zodiac in Sagittarius and Capricorn will and indeed must lead to fully conscious individuality, the anxious person who is bound to the material will cling fast to forms, hardening and crystallizing. In so doing the forces of destruction which dwell within matter will become effective, liberating encaptured life. We call this death.

The Sign Ruler Mars ♂

Scorpio is ruled both esoterically as well as exoterically by Mars. Mars as the double Ruler arouses the whole lower nature; in this way the life of the person born under Scorpio becomes an uninterrupted test, a struggle between the lower and the higher forces, between the innermost Being and the hardened Ego-forms. Through the double Mars rulership the genuine Scorpio type desires to partake of everything that life offers; he wishes to follow every love, every passion and every interest. He wishes to experience everything to the depths and is jealous of anything which might oppose his enjoyment of life. Whatever he has managed to gain hold of in this way he will not let go again; he wants to keep it forever. It is exactly here that the danger of excess lies, which must be suffered for. And the Scorpion is always suffering for it with ever new and painful losses. In so doing his love can turn to hate and his passion to abhorrence. He vacillates to and fro; on the one hand between new temptations and attractions of the world—spiritual as well as material—and on the other hand between aversion and grief, undecided to the last, doubting everything, loving life and desiring hungrily and yet rejecting.

Discord

This discord also has an inner counterpart: Scorpio fluctuates between good and evil and is often incapable of drawing a clear dividing line between these two forces. Indeed, the sign Scorpio lies between Libra and Sagittarius, the perfect YOU-orientation on the one hand and the impulse towards individual and spiritual freedom in Sagittarius on the other. This intermediate position brings in times of crisis a constant inner struggle which is called esoterically the "burning ground". This struggle can be all the more difficult because the instinctual nature of Man is considered to be a fatal weakness. The life of the senses and the sex life play a special role here, and the correct use of the sexual force can sometimes become a life problem.

In this connection both excesses and abstinence can cause psychological disturbances, completely cutting off contact to the surrounding world. "Virtue can all too easily become a vice"; this sometimes makes Scorpions fanatical or even neurotic in their behavior. Maintaining moderation in all things is difficult; thus, moderation becomes one of the most important tasks for the person born under Scorpio.

Conflict Between Life And Death

The leading thought of Scorpio is *triumph* or *becoming new*. It can also be expressed as "death *and* becoming", whereby in the case of a Scorpion the becoming is frequently overlooked and he loses himself in tearing himself to pieces, in accusing himself and in stinging himself. Scorpio in fact represents the entire polar tension between the forces of life and death which share the rulership. This causes a permanent conflict between death and life, between sensual enjoyment and denial, attraction and rejection, between hate and love, etc.

As the sign Scorpio always drives people to extremes, the danger thus lurks here of the dissolving powers predominating. If these drives, which Freud has described as the "death drives", urge towards this goal, then the struggle for life will flare up at the same time. Life and death will struggle for predominance. It is then a question of affirming the edifying forces of life, of renouncing doubting and pessimistic attitudes and of making an end of the "dying", of the "killing off" of so called lower tendencies. Not only the sexual drive can become a problem here, but also the ideas of purity and asceticism, which often in fact cause more problems.

The Esoteric Seed Thought Of Scorpio Runs:

Warrior I am, and from the battle I emerge triumphant.

Therefore, the victory, the becoming, the creatively positive must finally gain the upper hand. The continuously renewing abundance and continuity of becoming and of life must remove destructive, one-sided influences. Then the Scorpion will become a "triumphant disciple" who can follow the path to true individualization in Sagittarius.

After the purification, after the "dying" all diverging and dissolving forces must once again with the help of the will-power be collected together at the center and the purified Ego offered to the service of the world. Only with a strong Ego-nucleus, which arises out of the "burning, purifying fire" of Scorpio like a hardened diamond, can one help others in Sagittarius, in the "Light of the Soul", to follow the spiritual path and to put their own experiences to good use.

Spiritual Rebirth

Three animals symbolize the sign Scorpio: the snake, the scorpion, and the eagle or the phoenix. When the scorpion—with the poisonous sting which he can also turn against himself in self-destruction—gives way to his counterpart, the eagle or phoenix, which soars up out of the ashes with powerful wing beats to the greatest height, then the purified Scorpionic power will even work as a healing power. This is the spiritual rebirth, of which Scorpio is the sign. It is the vibration of a higher dimension which lifts him up to higher, spiritual fields from where whatever oppressed him returns to its place and troubles him no more. What he experiences breaks through when this inner light goes far beyond what his wordly and self-conscious Ego has up to now been aware of, and yet it arises from a reality which is within himself. It is the reality of his own Being. Within this nucleus of existence dwells the BEING which desires to manifest itself through him in the world. This eruption into the inner world is like a light in the darkness. One must open oneself to this light and allow it to have an effect. To this end we can prepare ourselves in today's meditation. This is in any case the meaning of every meditative exercise. The liberation and happiness which such contact with the innermost Being affords a person is usually a redeeming answer to the fundamental problems of human existence, to abandonment and doubt, to the struggle in the sign Scorpio. It is the triumph and the victory which can be achieved here.

Conversion, Change, Transmutation And Victory

Scorpio is the sign of inner change, of transmutation. It is the sign in which the lost son arises and returns to his father's home after having found nothing else which can satisfy him. It is this conversion which continuously brings dramatic moments in our lives when we recognize that we can never find real satisfaction in the external things of this life, but that we can only react correctly in unity with the innermost motivations of life. Once we have become aware of this unity of life in an illuminated moment or have experienced through a blow of fate the senselessness of purely external satisfaction, then we recognize, in the Scorpio month in particular, that we must strive by means of a new attitude for a fundamental change. This change is called the "Damascus Experience" in which "Saul became Paul". It usually begins when we let drop everything which has been established, with the renunciation of standardized, ossified life habits. This is an unusual demand on the Ego which clings to possessions and established things. And yet, the fulfillment of becoming new depends on this demand.

In this respect we must continuously break through the barriers which are always forming and tear the veil in order to reach the essential. We are again and again lapsing from our own inner center and falling back into the life forms of our little Ego; and everytime only a conversion, often a dangerous jump, will carry us back to the unity of life.

The jump into the innermost center sets in motion the process of death and becoming and requires the surrender, indeed often the destruction, of that which binds us to this world. This jump into nothing causes a continuously recurring anxiety in those born under Scorpion, for they know that they must one day make this jump. They know that they will have to give up everything, to lose everything—even themselves—in order to pass into this nothing, into dying. The anxiety about this nothing stands like a phantom in front of this great experience which is often conquered in a desperate and dramatic moment, yet usually only when there is no other escape.

After this great experience nothing else remains apart from the "I AM" which is not extinguished in this process of transmutation, but remains intact. After this inner transformation it remains the only reality which can really be experienced, rising like the phoenix from the ashes purified into life. That is the triumphant victory after the struggle. The Scorpion becomes the "triumphant disciple", as it is expressed in old texts; he is reborn out of the spirit.

The Demolition Of The "Little Self"

From the esoteric-psychological point of view the demolition of the "little self" preceeds this change or rebirth, although it was earlier built up with such love and expense. It must be transformed and demolished again so that the true structure of the inner Man can develop. This "Little Self" consists of the totality of all the evolved traits of personality which have arisen in the course of development. In the previous stage of development many so called "virtuous apparent Ego-forms" were built up; they are also called role-functions, and often have nothing to do with the innermost Being. It seems logical to wish to free oneself from bad habits, errors and vices; but that one must also give up the virtues, the successful role-functions or apparent rights brings the struggle between Soul and personality in Scorpio to the stage of rebellion. This process is very well illustrated in the Bhagavadgita when Aryuna is required by his Soul (Krishna) to kill both his enemies *and* his friends so that he can reach his Soul. Aryuna cannot understand this and suffers a breakdown in his carriage. This is the first crisis in Scorpio.

The transformation is a difficult but necessary process. It leads humanity in Scorpio to victory over the instinctual nature, over egoistic desires and goals. He becomes a "triumphant disciple" like Hercules, the Sun God, who won in this sign the gigantic victory over the nine-headed Hydra.

Keywords of the sign Scorpio are: testing, attempting, triumph.

The Threefold Tests In The Sign Scorpio

The testing in the sign Scorpio, according to Alice A. Bailey concern the three aspects of Man.

On the physical plane it is the sexual life and bodily comfort through egoistically established conditions of life as well as the money amassed for material purposes.
On the emotional plane it is fear, hate and ambition as driving motivations.
On the mental plane it is pride, separation, cruelty as hardening of the intellect.

This testing has nothing to do with anything which is set in motion by any kind of powers, but the spiritually developing person places himself in the determining circumstances where testing and disciplining are unavoidable and inevitable.

The "Dweller On The Threshold"

From the esoteric point of view the "Dweller on the Threshold" plays an important role in this testing and in the process of transformation and change. The Dweller on the Threshold is the totality of all psychic and spiritual factors which have not been subdued and which must finally be conquered or broken through before the inner light can reach full bloom. It is that part of the "Little Self" which opposes the forces of change. From the primeval depths of memory, from the deeply rooted past, experiences emerge which are the totality of all instinctual tendencies, of all inherited illusions and false intellectual attitudes, and of all psychic mechanisms. Every unmastered situation and every dominating error emerges on the surface of consciousness, and thus the struggle between pairs of opposites flares up. We are always exposed to this struggle between the person developing to consciousness and the Dweller on the Threshold, but in the sign Scorpio it reaches a dramatic climax.

The struggle with the Dweller on the Threshold is ended when we concentrate on the inner life, permitting growth of the Self. We can even support it by freeing ourselves from the previously mentioned obstructive factors on the three human planes: that is, if we work on ourselves constantly testing our actions and motives. This does not occur by suppressing false stimuli or through methods of compensation, but by realizing that the life in us is eternal movement and change and that we must become permeable for the finer emissions of the Soul. This leads to becoming one in the spiritual sense, whereby all negative reactions finally disappear by themselves and liberation through love becomes possible.

Out of this experience of unity an ever new becoming grows; from here creative, redeeming life force will flow towards us which tolerates no inertia, no tarrying in frictionless and harmonious peace or negative brooding.

The person who wanders on this path will again and again be stirred up by the life energies flowing through him so that he learns to live in harmony with his innermost Being, to serve selflessly and to co-operate in the tasks which are useful for the community or for humanity, because he can demand no more for his separated self.

Basic Exercise In Meditation

The whole process of the Scorpionic crisis-mechanics lies hidden in our basic exercise in meditation which today we wish to make more productive. It is the exercise in connection with the breath. You will remember: on exhaling we say "Let go"—"Relax", we hold our breath and say "Become one", on inhaling "Become new". And then "Be yourself" when we hold our breath again. We experience that in the constant releasing of oneself there lies a death, a renunciation of personal wishes, a submersion, a burial. In this "Let go" lies an acceptance of dying and at the same time the conquest of the small, earth-bound Ego. "Let go" leads to an awareness of a greater life and a deeper meaning in us. Thus in meditation death and becoming, death and resurrection, becoming one and becoming new are always taking place.

This inner attitude and exercise in meditation, carried out over months and years, transforms a person. It liberates the deep forces and lets them take effect. The healing power of rootedness in the intrinsic takes place. We attain in this way peace, detachment and freedom and emit these benevolently to our fellow men. Questions are solved effortlessly. Relationships lose their complications. The apparent Ego, the wordly Ego, the roles fall away; the Ego of existence breaks through. We release ourselves from the narrowness of Ego-mania and approach the great essentials of existence. We grow in basic confidence and from that position we can open ourselves anew to our fellow men and to the world. The heart expands; it becomes capable of love in a new way. More and more we approach in this attitude the foundation of our Being. Everything acquired, constructed, habits and false impressions of our childhood increasingly fall away. We penetrate to that deepest point where all the spiritual forces are still united within us in embryonic form. We stand in inner abundance. No person can be spiritually whole without being rooted in the absolute. To release oneself and to abandon oneself to fundamentals is the motivation of all religious life. It is comprehensive love which cares with self-abandonment for all life. It is the source of all Love from which we can serve strengthened and renewed. We arise from this source of Love, changed and purified, into becoming new. We have gained the victory and may cry out triumphantly "Be yourself". We ourselves have won the victory over dull matter. We ourselves have plunged into the purifying fire. We ourselves have flown up new and changed from the ashes like the phoenix. On inhaling we experience this soaring upwards into being oneself. We are born again in the spirit. Full of power and inner confidence we go courageously further along the way.

Today at the Full Moon we want to attune ourselves consciously to the manifesting forces of Light and Love, full of joy for all transformations, thus forming a shaft of light giving us and all doubting people courage and confidence once again in the indwelling forces of development which will lead us without fail to a better goal.

Thus we begin the meditation.

Scorpio Meditation

1. Stage: Preparation

We are sitting with a straight back. Our eyes are closed, but may open them occasionally if tensions arise. We rest our hands on our thighs; we may also open them, like two bowls; we place our feet together. We achieve the greatest relaxation of the body by transferring the inner focus to the middle of the body. We let the upper part of our body turn slightly in a circular motion until we have the sensation of sitting at the focal point, at the Hara.

Today we shall do the breathing exercise rather more fully in combination with the co-ordination of the threefold personality. For it expresses the Scorpio qualities in a special way.

2. Stage: Alignment

The alignment of the threefold personality with the Soul therefore occurs in combination with the basic exercise: "Let go, Relax, Become one, Become new, Be yourself". In so doing we use the Sacred Word OM after every one of these stages. First of all we breathe four times.

a) The physical body is relaxed. We are sitting on the chair and are borne by the chair, which is borne by the house, by the Earth. We become quite heavy and let go of everything which is in opposition to our true Being—above all each "small Ego" which has been formed in its role functions during the struggle for existence and which has falsified the inner Being, the Self. It is made up of protective and defensive attitudes, anxieties, feelings of inferiority, physical comforts, masks, ambition, demands and desires, unkindness, self-assertion, pride, detachment. By letting all this go, we prepare ourselves for recognizing our true Self, for accepting our existence and our fate.

OM

b) The emotional body is relaxed and calm as we relax confidently in our own depths. We descend into the soil of existence, we return to the Father's home; we leave behind everything that troubles us. We approach the Light in order to reach the area of radiation of BEING. We allow ourselves to be seized, changed and transformed by it. At the same time the relaxation signifies our movement into the all-embracing Love to which we humbly confide and surrender ourselves.

OM

c) The mental body becomes calm as we free ourselves from the thoughts which surround us. We look at them impartially. Then we direct our inner attention upwards. We see a white light and recognize our higher Self. We see a gulf which separates us from it. Suddenly we realize that, with our creative mind, we can bridge the gulf separating us from our true Being.

OM

d) Union With The Soul

We overcome the anxiety which is holding us back; we venture the leap into nothing, into the Light. In that moment when we surrender ourselves with a joyful heart and let go of our Ego the union with Being occurs. We open within and Being, the divine transcendence, flows into us. We are seized by the power of change and communion. We become open and transparent for the greater life within us, for greater thoughts and ideas which dissolve all our worries in a new light which flows through us into the world.

In the Becoming one lie the sources of a new life and of a new beginning in the sense "See, I make all things new". The Light of the Soul shines through our three bodies, purifying, strengthening and ennobling our life. In the Becoming new we ascend once again strengthened and blessed. The wheel of change on which we are swung from top to bottom and which has rested for a while at its deepest point now turns again; it raises us to new youthfulness, freshness and vital power so that we can fulfill our tasks, our duties and our service in the world.

OM

We wish to meditate on the Seed Thought:

Warrior I am, and from the battle I emerge triumphant.

3. Stage: Group Endeavor

Slowly we loosen our consciousness from our depths. We raise it to the highest point in the head, expand it over our immediate surroundings and join with those people around us, with all those people whom we should like to help. Then we say:

I am one with my group brothers,
and all what I have is theirs.
May the love of my Soul pour forth to them;
May the power, which is in me raise and lead them;
May the thoughts which my Soul creates reach and
encourage them.

We behold a path of light which stretches from humanity to that source where the Love of God dwells, which is expressed on our planet through Christ. We feel ourselves to be enclosed in this Love and dedicate the group to the service of the world. We slowly raise our hands and imagine how we all raise together a cup into the air in highly concentrated inner aspiration, in an appeal to the spiritual forces of Light and of Love which flow into our receptive consciousness—symbolically into the cup:

At the centre of all love I stand;
From that centre, I the Soul will outward move;
From that centre, I the one who serves will work.
May the love of the devine Self be shed abroad in my heart,
through my group and throughout the world.

4. Stage: Transmission To Humanity

By looking on the world of men in a visionary way, we allow the stream of energy of the "Great Invocation" to circle the Earth. In so doing we imagine how these powers radiate from numberless points of light and from a net of light spread out over our planet penetrating all areas of our planetary life, so that these spiritual energies can effect the events of the world, everywhere and at all times. We transmit the energy stream together to humanity through the Great Invocation.

From the point of Light . . .
(see page 234)

OM OM OM

Completion Of The Meditation

We open our eyes, breathe in and out deeply once, moving our head, our neck, our shoulders, our feet, our hands. Then we extend to each other our hands, look into each other's eyes and bow before each other.

SAGITTARIUS

Notes • The transition from Scorpio to Sagittarius • The symbol of Sagittarius • The arrow—higher purposefulness • Love of truth • Dogmatism • Three particular Sagittarian qualities • Concentration • Orientation • Impersonalness • The power of expansion • Polarity: Sagittarius-Gemini—Axis of thought • The urge to the far and wide • The esoteric seed-thought of Sagittarius • The ruler Jupiter • The esoteric ruler: The Earth • Intuition • Great motifs of life • The capacity for thought • The integration of the personality—individuation • Spiritual ascent • Sagittarius—Meditation •

SAGITTARIUS

SAGITTARIUS

Notes

Sagittarius	9th sign of the Zodiac
Month	23 November–21 December
Cross	Mutable
Temperament	Fire
Full Moon	Sun in Sagittarius Moon in Gemini
Houses	9th House/3rd House Axis of Thought
Problem Area	Opposition of individual thought and collective thought
Planetary Rulers	exoterically Jupiter esoterically Earth
Seed Thought	"I see the goal. I reach the goal and see another."

If we describe the qualities of Sagittarius, we do not want to do so in the usual sense, stating for example that Sagittarians love horses and like to make long journeys, or that they have a sharp intellect and tend to misuse this for disputations. No, we want to penetrate to those sources from which quite specific energy qualities are emitted which influence us and our planet Earth during the Sagittarius month, and above all seize hold of the individual whose Sun or Ascendant is in this sign.

The Transition From Scorpio To Sagittarius

In the sign Scorpio the egocentric Ego was recognized for what it was and placed where it belongs so that it cannot hinder the process of further development. The "small Ego" which was previously built up with so much love and expense must be dismantled, set free and transformed. For the personal, small Ego-consciousness it is always difficult to comprehend that it is not the only important and perfect thing which can live eternally. With each process of transformation it must realize that there is still something higher to be attained in further development and that the ability to withdraw from all petty, personal desires and egocentric efforts is necessary.

In the sign Sagittarius the struggle between the personality and the Soul is transposed to a higher spiral. The inner Light penetrates more intensely into the consciousness and spreads above all in the mind. The higher vision is illuminated so that one can even speak in certain cases of an intuitively enlightened mind. In Sagittarius independent thinking is really developed, free from collective norms, scales of measurement and egoistic goals. This flight into the superpersonal allows one to penetrate higher dimensions of the mind which recognize correct proportions and perceive the relationship between things, thus finding the right orientation and goals.

It is therefore necessary to adopt a superior stand point, indeed not only physically but also spiritually. It is precisely during the Sagittarius month that we should in all activities make efforts to free ourselves from the narrow confines of our personal life and to expand our spirit to higher spiritual planes. We should attempt to view our life from a higher "bird's eye" perspective in order to achieve the necessary distance from every day concerns and to grow into a spiritual dimension. It is once again the phoenix which rises from the ashes—purified through the Scorpionic forces of transformation—and which now in the Sagittarius month soar up to the greatest height, there to attain broader vision and individual freedom.

The Symbol Of Sagittarius ♐

In order to find the common denominator in considering the sign Sagittarius, we shall first study the symbols which represent it. One of the oldest and most well-known is the Centaur, that mythical being, half man and half horse. It symbolizes the Soul which is bound to the animal nature, identifying itself as it were with physicalness and its Egoness, with the desires and ambitions. Later this symbol was replaced by an archer on a white horse; the former no longer identifies himself with the animal and can therefore guide it more easily towards the goal of its efforts.

The symbol of Sagittarius which is most used at present and which most interests us, is the arrow; it points upwards and has on its bottom half a cross. The arrow is the sign of taking aim and shooting, for goal-conscious thinking and striving are so important for the person born under Sagittarius.

The Arrow—Higher Purposefulness

The arrow represents a further step in development; namely, becoming one with spiritual striving, which the Sagittarian shoots before him like an arrow. The arrow always flies towards a target and therefore symbolizes the fundamental quality of Sagittarius. He is always searching for new goals, for a new truth; he is never satisfied with what he has achieved; he is incessantly striving for greater realization.

After the Sagittarian has conquered the captivity in Scorpio and has gained the victory over the instinctual nature, he can venture out freely into the world with bow and arrow in search of new goals. The Sagittarian symbol expresses this quite clearly: the arrow which points into the distance, into the unknown, symbolizes the higher future, the vision of things to come, the goal lying in the wide unknown. The Sagittarian looks at the summit of life describing with great enthusiasm his goals, his ideas, his vision of the highest possibilities which the human spirit can attain. For this reason the Sagittarian often becomes a religious teacher, a philosopher, priest and teacher or wandering preacher. He co-operates in the creation of a new, spiritual, humane and ethical world, to which the improvement and ennobling of the human character belong. Although these ideals are still not full present reality and exist for the moment only in draft, in the mind, in anticipation, they give the whole life a new meaning, a new orientation and only in this way have an altering effect on the remaining forms of existence.

Love Of Truth

If the Sagittarian aims correctly then he shoots into the dark. This shows itself in life through a particular, and not always fortunate, love of truth. He finds it difficult to keep to himself a truth once he has recognized it; he would rather announce it to the whole world. And if these realizations or truths concern other people, he merely blurts them out with complete indifference without considering that he might hurt others. Indeed, he is even surprised when others take offense. Without malicious intention he can always lay his finger on the sore point or on the essential aspect of a matter or of a person. He will always get into difficulties in this way with the world until he learns the right dosage through the wise use of his intellect.

He will then use his judgment and spiritual power only according to the concepts of moderation and correctness and in each case he will have to avoid hurting or damaging others. The motif of assistance and the sense of justice of the developed Sagittarian will ensure that no excessive hardness arises.

Dogmatism

If the personality of the Sagittarian is not yet mature, the little Ego will still vibrate too strongly, and the Sagittarian will then become dogmatic. Only his own opinion is valid, he will always want the last word and he will attempt, with all the rhetorical ability which is at his command, to push through his own point of view. In so doing he runs the danger of representing the injustice, committed and recognized by himself, to the outside world as justice, so adjusting things that they appear to be the truth. Sometimes he even knows how, with outwardly clever eloquence, to turn his own weaknesses into a philosophy in order to disguise in this way his true motives. He justifies the satisfaction of private desires or ambitious plans with sound philosophical reasons against which one can scarcely argue. Thus the Sagittarian becomes a demagogue.

In order to be able to maintain appearances before the world, he finds it difficult to admit that he is wrong. He easily loses himself in complicated trains of thought, sitting on a high horse and looking contemptuously down at others. These are some of the negative sides of Sagittarius which must be mentioned for the rounding off of the picture.

Three Particular Sagittarian Qualities

We have now approached the essence of Sagittarius a little closer. Three qualities have crystallized clearly which comprise the essence of this sign in its qualitative sense and which can be summarized in three concepts:

1. Concentration and orientation
2. Control of the forms of personality
3. Expansion and development

This also corresponds to the technique of using a bow and arrow in Zen Buddhism. The disciple holds the arrow in concentration; he identifies with the target and summons all his powers; that is concentration and orientation. At this moment he must dispense with his "small Ego", which is only possible through the perfect control of his personality. He learns to relax in tension. Only when he has reached this state, is he able to shoot the arrow, which is similar to an expansion and a development.

Concentration

Thus the first step has been made in the power of *concentration* which enables us to discipline our mind and speech and to cut out the many external diversions and thoughts. This power can best be expressed with the words of an ancient wise man who had the following to say about the way one should speak. "Beware of the fool whose volume of words is enough for ten men. He shoots off a hundred arrows and each one is wide of the target. If you are wise, shoot one and the correct one". Speaking is indeed a great art, and concentration is the key to it. But the control of speech does not only lie in the wise use of words outwardly, but also in the control of the many voices which come from within and which often prevent us from hearing the "voice of silence".

Orientation

If a person succeeds through concentration in disciplining his mind and speech, then that typical Sagittarian characteristic develops which is called a *sense of orientation*. This sense takes care of the potential ability of Man to find the right way through the dense undergrowth of human insufficiency—that way which leads to the true Self. This hidden, inner center should be the target at which our arrow is aimed. If we listen with all our senses to the inner voice of our Self, follow with the greatest sensitivity and inner flexibility the lead of our intuitions, we shall find our way and at the same time develop the ability to recognize the way for others and for the whole of humanity.

Impersonalness

At the next stage it is necessary to cultivate those Sagittarian energies which make us capable of putting the "small Ego" of our personality in its place, where it will no longer hinder further development; thus the Sagittarian will become free for striving after spiritual goals. It is that superpersonal attitude of mature and wise people which is frequently described as selflessness or *inoffensiveness*.

We can practice this ability by adopting the attitude of an observer, distancing ourselves from ourselves as far as possible so that we can see ourselves speaking, thinking, feeling and behaving. This process is accelerated by the third and fundamental energy force which flows through Sagittarius: the *power of expansion*.

The Power Of Expansion

It is the power which is always driving a person forward, which enables him to leave age behind him and to look for new opportunities, which forces him to ask after the great WHY and WHITHER, searching incessantly, and which finally conveys to him in stages the revelations of the secrets of nature and of the Universe. One can interpret the concept "expansion" in different ways. In esoteric philosophy expansion is a fundamental principle which penetrates the whole Cosmos and which brings to all living creatures at all stages the impulse-giving power for further development. This concerns us human beings in the first instance with regard to the development of our consciousness, of our mind, of the alertness of our senses and of the intensified ability of perception. Every expansion of our human horizon is at the same time an expansion of our consciousness and thus a development.

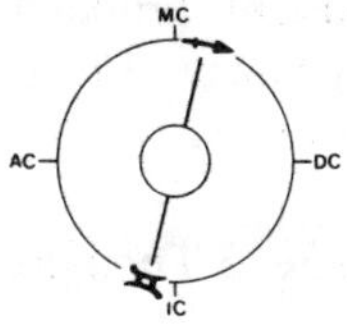

Polarity: Sagittarius-Gemini
Axis of Thought

The power of expansion or the consciousness-expanding principle is particularly effective on the Sagittarius-Gemini axis of polarity. We shall call it the Axis of Thought. It brings with it the contrast between rational, concrete knowledge and superordinated, meaningful contemplation, between the collective mind and the individual mind, between the close and the far, between the everyday and the special, etc.

In the sign Gemini the power of expansion spurs on the urge to further education, to the amassing of knowledge and thus promotes the development of the rational mind, of the intellect; whereas in Sagittarius it stimulates self-observation, one's own mind and judgement and thus enables one to form one's own picture of the world.

Ths axis can also be described as a path from "the intellect to the intuition", from the small Ego to the Soul, from the Ego bound to the Collective, to free individuality. It is that power, effective on the Axis of Thought, which leads to true self-becoming, which gives access to universal consciousness and which reveals the secrets of the Plan of evolution.

The polar tension between Sagittarius and Gemini is the reason why Sagittarius is continuously running up against the boundaries and barriers which have been imposed on him by his upbringing and the norms of behavior of the Collective. In his urge for expansion he would like to exceed these; he would like to escape from everyday obligations, social confines, family traditions in order to participate in an ever larger world. His individual urge for freedom makes him energetically reject every constraint. He seeks freedom and a form of life suitable to himself. In so doing he is always penetrating the borders of knowledge, thus entering the darkness of the unconscious as well as the light of the superconscious.

If too much resistance is used to oppose the urge towards room to move and towards freedom, then the internal dynamism has an effect on the "small Ego". The Ego-nucleus becomes hardened, and the Sagittarian will be in danger of becoming conceited and thus arrogant and proud.

The Urge To The Far And Wide

The longing for the far and wide and for unlimited freedom will always remain an inner characteristic of Sagittarius. In this way there is something restless, inconstant, brilliantly varied about his life; a "certain something" is always driving him on. He never has any peace; he needs change and variety so that he can develop.

The Esoteric Seed Thought Of Sagittarius

I see the goal. I reach the goal and see another.

"The Sagittarian must fly from place to place to seek and to find the arrow which he has loosed", as it is expressed in ancient texts. In this way he learns a great variety of things, broadening his horizons and arriving at his own conclusions, at his own convictions and view of the world.

Thus constant progress becomes a central principle of Sagittarius. He is restlessly and uninterruptedly in search of the ultimate truth, but often aware at the same time that he will never find it. It is the conflict between the absolute and ideal goal on the one hand and the real and attainable one on the other which torments him and drives him on at the same time in the constant process of growth.

The Ruler Jupiter ♃

In accordance with his ruling planet Jupiter the character of the Sagittarian is jovial, just and loyal. He is a true lover of humanity and knows what others need. Basically they have a genuinely happy nature and are often real lovers of life. They wish to affirm life and are therefore filled with an often ungrounded optimism.

Genuine Sagittarians get along with all sorts of people wherever they are and in every situation of life, and they adjust themselves as best they can to all circumstances. As Sagittarius belongs to the Mutable Cross, he knows how to accept things as they are; so long as his principles and the above-mentioned truths are not threatened, he is always adaptable to any circumstance. He is also personally very pleasant and takes a keen interest in the welfare of his fellow men. For this reason he also likes to protect the weak and to mediate in conflicts, encouraging and educating.

Jupiter allows the Sagittarian to hold on to a higher vision, to a goal that is to be attained and enables him to describe it in vivid images. How it is to be reached, he himself often does not know, for he too must first find the way. But he holds on firmly to the vision he has beheld working tirelessly for it in his thoughts. He dreams of a better future setting out to look for it and to find it. He describes it in detail and incites others to adopt his ideals by similarly engaging themselves in the general improvement of the world.

The Esoteric Ruler: The Earth ⊕

The esoteric Ruler of the sign Sagittarius is the Earth. Here the Earth appears for the first time as an influence. It is logical that the Earth, which is a planet like all the others, should also exert a specific influence. The qualitative tone of the Earth, corresponding to the Seventh Ray according to Alice A. Bailey, is the Third Ray of active intelligence. Therefore, the intelligence will also be unfolded to the maximum extent in Sagittarius, not the intellect as in the opposite sign Gemini, but the intuition which comes from the all-perceiving, elevated position which the Sagittarian tries to attain. Through the influence of the Earth as the Principle of Reality his thoughts and opinions must also stand the test of hard reality. They should not remain castles in the air. The Earth pulls him back down to reality, both through the hard struggle for existence as well as through the fact that he is actually "in love" with this world. That is why he becomes a true teacher able to effect the world as educator and enlightener.

Intuition

The Sagittarian loves and cherishes his visions, ideas and ideals until an opinion, a philosophy, a usable structure of thought arises out of them, which he can pass on full of conviction. A further interesting effect of this visionary world of imagination of the Sagittarian is that the thoughts which he has emitted endeavor to return to him again. Just as he himself likes to move off on his travels to collect knowledge and then to bring what he has learned home again, so his thoughts do exactly the same. It is the "returning arrow of intuition", as it is expressed esoterically, which expresses itself through a bright ray of light in the intuitive and concentrated attitude of the Sagittarian, by which means he can bring light into the darkest affairs.

Great Motifs Of Life

In accordance with the Fire temperament Sagittarius is an intuitive sign. It is therefore important for us during the Sagittarius month to pay attention to our inspiration, to re-examine our visions, ideas and ideals and carry the best of the past into the present and the future. One can call back into consciousness great motifs of life, ideals about life which have already been a cause of inspiration and were perhaps direction pointers for the future. These motifs can become new sources of life, bestowing that sound optimism and vital Will which had perhaps been lost in Scorpio.

We can now perceive and cultivate once again faith and trust in the future in spite of possible oppressing experiences.

The innermost law of Sagittarius is orientation and direction. We are able to return to the starting point to find there once again the Light, the impulse and the forward striving motif which once used to drive us on. Once we have discovered it, it will fill us with new power reviving us anew. Then we shall occupy ourselves with striving after better, spiritual opportunities, with forgetting the old and with coming to terms with what has been established, with blows of fate suffered, with errors, idleness, unfulfilled desires, etc. That is of inestimable value for our further development and for a meaningful life; for a faith in the future imbued with optimism and the deepest conviction, a faith in a better world, with sufficient power and endurance take on form attracting the corresponding spiritual and material values.

The Capacity For Thought

For the developed Sagittarian the capacity for thought is the most important tool for acting effectively in the world. During this period we are able to comprehend that thought is an instrument with which we should behave conscientiously, for "thought is power". With sufficient intensity it takes on form; it torments or delights us. In order to learn in the Sagittarius month how to treat this valuable instrument properly and to arrive at our own thoughts, a certain detachment and distancing from the hackneyed thought forms constantly whirring around us is necessary. Every process of recognition requires that we distance ourselves, that we withdraw, so that a matter can be seen objectively and so judged.

The difficulty of thinking independently is often connected with the fact that we have not disassociated ourselves from acquired opinions. We are repeatedly experiencing how we are unable to free ourselves from a worry or anxiety; it is constantly circling about us and will no longer let us go, sometimes it even takes on gigantic proportions. Thought is a powerful force which influences our Ego and has corresponding consequences. Thought is an energy which we can use very effectively for creating a new structure for our Being, but also for building a new and better world around us.

It has been said, "energy follows thought" and "a man is what he thinks". It therefore depends on my thinking and on my attitude whether I am good, bad, successful or happy. Everything that happens to me is born beforehand in the realm of the spirit, of the mind. In this sense I am myself responsible, I am "the smith of my own happiness". It is therefore important that we learn to think in the right way and that we realize the useful application of the power of thought. A prerequisite for this however is a certain degree of inner freedom. Anyway, the concept of freedom plays an important role not only for one's own thoughts but also for self-becoming in Sagittarius. We must first of all become aware that we have the possibility of free thought and free decision.

The Integration Of The Personality—Individuation

In the sign Sagittarius the freedom of the decision of the Will through one's own thought begins to develop, and thus the process of individuation is introduced. We must not forget here that the person who wants to come into contact with his Soul must first of all have achieved uniqueness and identity through the integration of his threefold nature. One of the most important means for attaining this is correct thinking and the application of the spiritual energy of the Will. Through infallible goal-orientation we can unite the various elements of the human psyche, organize and integrate it and turn it into a functional unity. Correct thought in connection with self-perception is therefore particularly possible in the sign Sagittarius.

Sagittarius is the last Fire sign in the Zodiac. All Fire signs are concerned with individualization and self-becoming. We remember: the impulse for manifestation was first emitted in Aries, there the process of development always has its beginning. In Leo we can present ourselves as we perceive ourselves, and show ourselves to the world as we are. Sagittarius is concerned with processes of consciousness. Here one experiences oneself as a thinker in the sense, "I think, therefore I am".

In Sagittarius we too find that our own mind and our free ability to make decisions are self-evident. We can no longer imagine how it could have been otherwise. We stand up for our own convictions with complete competence having the courage for our own individual trains of thought and liberating ourselves in this way more and more from the collective function of the Superego. Even if at the outset we place ourselves in opposition through our own individual opinions to traditional views, it nevertheless does not make much difference if we still stand up for what we believe to be right, even if we receive no recognition for doing so. It even gives us pleasure to live as we think. If we begin to live more consciously—and in this respect Sagittarius is a help to us—then we shall also be happier, for we know what we are doing. To a certain extent we shall come into the full possession of our powers—and that makes us freer.

Spiritual Ascent

Thus, a spiritual ascent lies hidden in Sagittarius which can lead to true self-becoming, to initiation in Capricorn, to a more elevated position from where life and its bustle can be observed, where one is raised above things and nothing more can disturb one because one has gained a better view of the world and has discovered the meaning behind everything. The Sagittarian is no longer wandering in the dark because he knows what he must do.

A ray of light falls on problems, one recognizes the cause, the causal relationship, one perceives a distant, but possible, image of the attainable. From the light of intuition arises the dazzling and constant Light of the Soul which illuminates the mind and produces that unity which is called esoterically "the merging of the two Lights, of the Greater and of the Lesser". It is the Light of the personality which unites with the Light of the Soul. Here thought plays an important role. It is a matter of approaching the true inner image of Man, of becoming one with the Soul. We want to aim our power of thought at this goal which now becomes powerful at the Sagittarius Full Moon.

Sagittarius Meditation

Preparation

We are sitting with a straight back. Our eyes are closed, but may open occasionally if tensions arise. We rest our hands on our thighs, we place our feet together. We achieve the greatest relaxation of the body by transferring the inner focus to the middle of our body. We let the upper part of our body turn slightly in a circular motion until we have the sensation of sitting at the focal point, at the Hara.

The breath also has a part to play in the preparation for the meditation. The peace, relaxation and collectedness which emanates from our bodily attitude is increased by combining four words with four breaths. On exhaling we say "Let go—Relax", then we hold our breath and say "Become one", on inhaling we say "Become new", on holding our breath "Be yourself". We do this a few times.

1. Stage: Depth Relaxation

We slowly let our attention in our head wander down between our jaws—through our neck and into the upper breast. Here we allow it to rest for a moment. Slowly our focal point slides down further from the upper breast into the middle of the body, behind the breast bone, to the level of the heart. After a time we let the focal point sink further from the end of the breast bone down to the waist, behind the navel to the lower part of the body and on to the base of the spine. We pump down some air and press against the chair.

2. Stage: Alignment

After each of the three stages we use the Secret Word OM in order to expel disturbing vibrations.

a) The Physical Body

I am here, fully present, here on the chair, in this room, at this hour, with these people. I am sitting on the chair. The chair is borne by the house, the house by the Earth, the Earth by the planet, the planet through the cosmic laws of gravitation. This conformity makes my life secure. I am carried, secure. I expand my consciousness, I can see the Earth, the horizon, the whole sphere of the planet. My body is a part of the Earth, of this planet. When I die, it will return to the Earth, but I shall remain.

I dedicate my physical body to the service of the Soul.

OM

b) The Emotional Body

I concentrate on the heart center. I have an emotional body through which I have desires—desires for love, for understanding, for peace, for happiness. My neighbor has the same desires and feelings. I can extend my emotional body to my fellow men, to my family, to my group, to all people in the town in which I live—to the whole nation in which I live. I expand my consciousness out over the borders of my nation to other nations. They are all human beings like you and I. I can see the people in America, in Europe, in Russia, in China, in Africa; other races and other peoples, but they are all human beings like myself. I identify in love with all humanity of which I am but a tiny part. I dedicate my emotional body to the service of humanity.

OM

c) The Mental Body

Then I raise my consciousness into my head, first of all to the center of the brain and then into the center between the eyebrows. My eyelids are relaxed. I can see thoughts flowing through my brain; they come from all directions; they are all around me; they penetrate me like an uninterrupted stream of thoughts. Yet I myself remain at the center observing them; I look on them as children at play. I can direct the focus of my consciousness towards one of these thoughts flowing through me; I approach it, draw it to me, consider it more closely, reflect on it. But I can also identify with it penetrating deeply into it in order to grasp its meaning.

I only think what I really want to, what I affirm from my innermost being. I consistently reject all destructive, negative thoughts—thoughts of worry, annoyance, suffering, doubt. I only think positive, edifying thoughts which are good for me, for my fellow men, for all human beings. I only desire the very best, both in thought and speech as well as in accomplishment. I dedicate my capacity for thought to the benefit of all Mankind.

OM

3. Stage: Sagittarius Visualization Exercise

I am standing in endless space under a dark night sky. Deep silence envelops me. I am alone. I can see before me a shining white star towards which I move with determination. I reach it and see behind it another star towards which I move in turn.

We meditate on the Seed Thought:

I see the goal. I reach the goal and see another.

Then I listen into myself. I hear a faint tone sound within me, calling me. Like the ray of a search light I collect my thoughts and direct them like an arrow down into my own depths. There I behold a white pure light with which I merge. The light spreads over my whole body penetrating my pores and forming around me a shining aura.

Then we say together the Mantram of the Disciple:

I am a point of light within a greater Light.
I am a strand of loving energy within the stream of Love divine.
I am a point of sacrificial Fire, focused within the fiery Will of God.
And thus I stand.
I am a way by which men may achieve.
I am a source of strength, enabling them to stand.
I am a beam of light, shining upon their way.
And thus I stand.
And standing thus, revolve
And tread this way the ways of men,
And know the ways of God.
And thus I stand.

4. Stage: Group Endeavor

Then we raise our consciousness into our head and extend it lovingly to the people here in the room. We join with all those who approach the spiritual energies at the Full Moon in meditation, forming a group unity on the mental plane receptive to the cosmic energies of the sign Sagittarius.

We imagine how we all raise together a cup in highly concentrated inner aspiration and attunement to the spiritual forces of Light and of Love which flow into our receptive consciousness—symbolically into the cup. We slowly raise our hands.

We behold a path of light which stretches from humanity to that source where the Love of God dwells, which is expressed on our planet through Christ. We feel ourselves to be enclosed in this Love and dedicate the group to the service of the world.

At the centre of all love I stand;
From that centre, I the Soul will outward move;
From that centre, I the one who serves will work.
May the love of the devine Self be shed abroad in my heart,
through my group and throughout the world

We slowly lower our hands.

5. Stage: Transmission To Humanity

Now we turn to Mankind letting the needs, worries and burdens of men flow into us, raising them to the Light of the Soul and praying for help from that source.

We allow the living stream of the energy of Light, Love and creative Will to flow out through us. In so doing we imagine how these powers radiate from numberless points of light and from a net of light out over our planet penetrating all areas of our planetary life, so that these spiritual energies can effect the events of the world everywhere and at all times.

We transmit the energy stream together to humanity through the Great Invocation.

From the point of Light . . .
(see page 234)

Completion Of The Meditation

We open our eyes, breathe in and out deeply once, moving our head, our neck, our shoulders, our feet, our hands. Then we extend to each other our hands, look into each other's eyes and bow before each other.

CAPRICORN

Notes • The transition Sagittarius-Capricorn •
The symbol of Capricorn • Characteristics of the Capricorn type •
The strong and weak Ego • Fully conscious individuality •
Negative self-consciousness—The despot •
Matured authority • Peak experience •
The polar tension: Capricorn-Cancer—the axis of individuality •
The ruler Saturn • The esoteric seed thought of Capricorn •
Responsibility • The will • The awakening of the will •
The crises of Capricorn • The knee and initiation •
Transformation in motifes • The plan of evolution •
The inner light—Christ-Consciousness • Capricorn-Meditation.

CAPRICORN

CAPRICORN

Notes

Capricorn	10th sign of the Zodiac
Month	22 December–20 January
Cross	Cardinal
Temperament	Earth
Full Moon	Sun in Capricorn Moon in Cancer
Houses	10th House/4th House Axis of Individuality
Problem Area	Opposition of the Individual and the Collective
Planetary Ruler	exoterically Saturn esoterically Saturn
Seed Thought	"Lost am I in light supernal, yet on that light I turn my back."

The sign Capricorn occupies the highest point of the Zodiac. It represents the summit of human development, the highest spiritual goals which a human being can achieve. It also signifies the final stage of a development and the beginning of a new period; astrologically a new quadrant and spiritually a new state of consciousness. In this respect we think of the change from the Old to the New Year which always occurs in the sign Capricorn.

The Transition Sagittarius-Capricorn

In the sign Sagittarius Man obtained through his own efforts Ego-consciousness which is capable of independent thought and which begins to form its own picture of the world from a variety of possibilities. In Capricorn, an Earth sign on the Cardinal Cross of the Will, there is an addition the energy of the Will. Here known truths are tested in reality; they arrive at a process of fermentation, they are built, steel-like and hardened into the character and form the autonomous rules of life to which the individuality conforms.

In a spiritual sense the Cardinal sign Capricorn is a symbol of the initiation in which spiritual power and authority are attained through the energy of the Will and Man frees himself from foreign influences and external constraint. However, this is only possible with a developed self-consciousness, the basis for which are the ability to think and to comprehend for oneself as well as an independent philosophy of life and an ethic which were developed in Sagitarrius.

To some extent the expansion of the consciousness which was attained in Sagittarius is stabilized in Capricorn. Esoteric writings also express the process of initiation as a "stabilization of consciousness". This becomes evident in Capricorn in the form of an integrated and finished individuality, in other words one which evolves from within itself. The evolution of Self and individualization depend on a well functioning Will, for the Will combines the various elements of human nature into a functional unity and causes the integration of remoulding of the personality. All potential abilities and achievements, as well as all unwelcome states, are prompted, developed or discarded by the vitalizing, consciously directed power of the Will until a refined and perfected form evolves which corresponds to the true inner Self.

However, this process can only come fully into effect when the individual has developed his Ego-center and knows that he himself is the carrier of this special freedom of the Will. If the Ego-center of the individual is weak, then the integrating or synthesizing energy of the Will cannot become effective; the evolution of consciousness of one's own Self fails.

The Symbol Of Capricorn ♑

All processes of self-actualization begin with the consolidation of a supportive, resistent Ego-center. This is also expressed by the symbol of Capricorn in which the circle is completed and its contents compressed into the narrowest space, thus forming a nucleus of crystallization as an extract of all earlier experiences. The Saturnine Capricorn force draws everything to itself, concentrating, centralizing, collecting and conserving what has already been established, moulding a firm structure which is hard and resistent, forming essences. It is therefore capable of achieving with these concentrated energies of unity and Will incisive and profound results.

Characteristics Of The Capricorn Type

The accumulation of his own Ego-powers often makes the Capricorn type egoistic. Full of ambition, he wants to outdo others and will tolerate no one as his equal. He alone wishes to possess power in order to triumph over others, or to enjoy the pleasures of achievement.

He is always climbing to the top. He can find no peace below. Just as the mountain goat climbs to the highest summit, so the Capricorn type strives towards the highest summit of human existence. In so doing the preparation for the ascent always assumes an important place. It is not a matter of passing from one day to the next. He needs plenty of time for everything; everything must be thoroughly thought through beforehand. The greatest care and caution are expended so that nothing unforeseen can interfere. "Good work takes time" is his motto.

The Capricornian has indefatiable energy, tenacity and a willingness to work—qualities which often enable him to bring apparently hopeless tasks to completion in spite of every opposition. Obstacles spur him on to greater achievements. The Capricorn type is also very strict with himself. He is the typical "Iron Man of Duty". This performance of duty, behavior according to rigid rules, often makes him hard and unfeeling to those around him. In order to preserve his respect and prestige he frequently suppresses all warmth of feeling. The drive towards ever higher positions, ever greater personal power and far-reaching influence acts as an incentive and often causes him to neglect emotional commitments. The Capricornian can be very egoistic in such matters—or at least we feel that he is.

The Strong And Weak Ego

The notion that this type of egoism indicates a particularly strong Ego is incorrect. In such cases the Ego is certainly overemphasized but not secure, for it needs recognition and confirmation on the part of society, the feeling of professional eminence or of apparent spiritual superiority and of personal power.

However, whoever is in full possession of a well-developed Ego, ruled by the Self, does not have need of the crutch of such egoisms. People with a self-consciousness which has developed from within itself are flexible, at peace with themselves, needing no confirmation from without. They are tolerant and understanding of others. People with a weak Ego on the other hand always feel that their basic rights are under threat from others and are therefore always on the defensive. They build up their position and secure themselves on all sides. So as to enable their own personalities to appear strong, they establish relations with the most influential people possible and always want to be pulling the strings. It is normally sufficient for them to exercise their power in a concealed manner.

Fully Conscious Individuality

A person however who has matured to fully conscious individuality has no need of these kinds of prestige-aid. He is able to make the conscious, individual decision to place his strong and free personality at the disposal of the service of the Collective. An authority which has matured to such an extent has not been liberated for its own advantage but for the service of its fellow men. Such a person resists indoctrination and unconsidered imitation of collective norms or social status seeking. On his own free account, on his own responsibility, from the view point of his lofty position he looks for new ways of solving the problems of Mankind. Without regard for worldly esteem and position he dares to assume individuality because he can act according to his awakened world conscience.

Negative Self-Consciousness—The Despot

Thus, the Capricornian who has achieved a high degree of consciousness does not sun himself in the full exercise of his powers, does not become proud, placing himself through hardened egoism above others, forcing them to submit to his Will, for this would be the picture of a tyrant, a despot and the negative expression of a strong personality. It shows the person who holds fast with all his might to his position in the world, to his throne and to his status, and who is unable, through wise foresight, to concede to others, to younger forces. He hangs on with iron energy to old principles and habits simply because they have helped him to success and to his elevated position. Even when he realizes that he is behaving incorrectly, that young and dynamic new forces are pushing upwards, he defends his position with all his powers.

Matured Authority

The insight that one should withdraw, the ability not to misuse power and to find it, not in a successful position, but in inner authority requires the genuine spiritual greatness of a secure personality which has matured from within itself. Calmness, cheerfulness and kindness have been from time immemorial the hall-marks of a mature authority experienced from within itself. It does not support itself by power and wealth, but solely by the inner omnipotence of a humanly, professionally and really superior personality. Genuine authority is founded on self-evident effects, on subconscious vibration and not on external manipulation. Whoever has achieved such inner maturity will at the summit use the position of power he has attained for the benefit of others and to help them in turn to reach their maximum potential.

Peak Experience

The spiritually awakened person sets out alone, and usually in opposition to the norms and goals of the Collective, in order to strive for the highest pinnacle of his spiritual abilities. Once he has attained the summit, he stands in the full Light. All the great experiences on mountain summits reported in the Bible are connected with Capricorn. Moses the Law Giver on Mount Sinai is Saturn in Capricorn imposing the law of karma on people. The Mount of Transfiguration in the New Testament is Venus in Capricorn. Here Love, Mind and the Will meet in the person of Christ who was transfigured for all Mankind. At the same time he received the vision of the Plan and knew what he had to do.

We know of other "peak experiences" from the tradition of the great Mystics who in the utmost spiritual concentration, meditation or contemplation with the inner Will for existence or for the pure motif of Love have achieved spiritual awakening and unity.

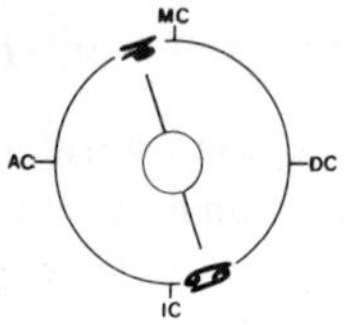

The Polar Tension: Capricorn-Cancer
The Axis Of Individuality

The opposite force of the sign Cancer is activated through the Capricorn experience. In the process of initiation we are stretched out so to speak on the polar axis of the Collective and the individual, that is to say, we must unite these two poles within ourselves. That means in practice that when we have achieved the summit of self-experience in Capricorn, then we must turn again to humanity, approaching the Collective from the other side of the axis of individuality in the sign Cancer.

These two poles are at the same time identical with the polarity of the father (Capricorn) and the mother (Cancer) which merge in the experience of individuation or in the initiation into unity. Cancer represents the gateway to physical birth and Capricorn the gateway to spiritual birth or initiation. During the Capricorn period the "gateway to the spiritual world is wide open", more open than during the Summer time in the sign Cancer. An intensive spiritual impulse is particularly perceptible at the time of the Capricorn Full Moon which arouses people to contemplation and spiritual reflexion. The days of Christmas with their Festival of Christ are the period in which Christ was born. Every year this is a period affording the opportunity for an inner spiritual rebirth through which one will be initiated into the mysteries of life.

This rebirth can occur when a person goes through experiences of solitude, which each individual consciousness must experience. Yet, in this experience of solitude the Will awakens to unity because the heart longs in the iron coldness of "isolated oneness" (Capricorn) for love and warmth (Cancer). That is one of the reasons why people come together at Christmas to celebrate the Festival of Christ with each other. If the desire for attachment and safety is strong enough, it will breach the walls and break up the embittered, self-confining pride of Capricorn. Once the need for solitude has been suffered, then Love awakens in the heart once again.

We too can go through such experiences in the Capricorn month and be thankful for every friendly word, for sympathy and attention, for every human consideration. We can liberate ourselves from the fortress of the Ego, from our isolation, embitteredness and inner coldness, setting out once again in search of Love as the most precious of human possessions. We shall realize that without Love we should only be intelligent robots. A person must frequently go through such experiences of solitude so that he may arrive at this understanding.

The Ruler Saturn ♄

Saturn is both the esoteric and the exoteric Ruler of Capricorn, the planet of crystallization and of form. On the physical plane it shows itself as the setter of limits, as the great Educator. In the spiritual development of the consciousness it keeps us, as the "Guardian of the Threshold", from steps which can only be trod unscathed with a secure sense of reality.

In Capricorn there are three experiences, that of the valley, that of the plane and that of the summit or transfiguration. In Capricorn a person certainly stands with both feet on the ground, but can at the same time freely run around and scale the heights of worldly ambition or spiritual aspiration. When he has attained the summit of his desires and expansion has reached its greatest extent, then the influence of Saturn takes effect. Then the skin forms which conserves the new entity; the crystal-hard, refined form arises at the final phase of every development. This is the symbol of the firmly closed personality, of fully conscious individuality through which the Soul can act, dedicating itself to the inner Light, to the Plan or to the service of humanity. This transfiguration is called the "Transfiguration on the Mountain". Saturn becomes the "Great Initiator" leading a person to a wholly new consciousness of himself and of his purpose in life, which indeed represents a part of the Plan.

However, if the crystallization has reached a certain degree of imperviousness and hardness, it easily becomes negative manifesting itself in egoism and a materialistic outlook, or, on the spiritual plane, as the experience of the loneliness of a self-confined, individual unity. But it is on just this rigid form that the Capricornian must test his powers if he wishes to penetrate to the essence of all things. He must allow the self-erected form to become transparent and must crack the hardened shell if he is to penetrate to the essential, to the true Self. Saturn therefore represents the setter of limits, the crust or skin, and from the esoteric point of view the "Guardian of the Threshold" which the Capricornian will come up against, both physically and with his consciousness, and which he must overcome. At the same time however Saturn is the "Great Initiator" who opens for us the gateway to higher consciousness once all the lessons have been learned, all tests passed and all debts paid.

Furthermore, Saturn is always the sign of the ending of a process. The symbol for this is the mountain summit. Esoterically this is called "a periodic resting or interruption" because no further ascent is possible. Once a person has descended again into the "Valley of Life", only then will he be able to undertake a fresh attempt.

The Esoteric Seed Thought of Capricorn Runs:

Lost am I in light supernal, yet on
that light I turn my back.

As we have seen, the crisis arises when the summit which we appeared to have reached must be given up in order to bring the Light which we have found there to Mankind, whom we are to show in turn the way to the summit. Therefore, during the Capricorn month we should undertake with great determination never to stay still in the position we have already reached, not to believe that we have already achieved or accomplished everything that there is to be done, but rather to willingly follow the rhythmic energies of life and to descend once again to convey the knowledge and Light we have found to others. We can develop our energy of Will and our capacity for Will in order to apply them for the common benefit of all humanity. Wherever we meet abuses, we should feel ourselves called upon to work for their removal.

Responsibility

The world conscience awakens when a person arrives at complete self-actualization. It is the consciousness of a Soul acting through an integrated personality and always thinking and behaving according to large, broad concepts of oneness. Thus, as a transfigured personality permeated by the Soul or as a self-conscious person one can no longer say, "that's got nothing to do with me, let others get on with it". No, here we must co-operate with the Plan of evolution, accepting responsibility for the greater whole, for the community. We must apply our small will-power with joy and enthusiasm, not only for the creation of correct human relations and ordered relationships for all but also for the establishment of common human rights.

The Will

From the esoteric point of view it is the application of the spiritual energy of Will which leads the Capricornian to balance egoistic Ego-hardening with humanly acceptable responsibility. He himself must desire to descend from his throne; he himself must apply his Will for the benefit of the community; he himself must undergo in the profoundest despair the inner transformation. No one can tell him this, for he will not listen to such advice, however well-intentioned. In Capricorn the power of the Will becomes mighty. Therefore, only he himself can decide on a change of motives or on an inner conversion. Thus, we are told, the evolved, self-conscious individual in the final analysis initiates himself.

The Capricorn can activate his Will and direct it at chosen targets. Whether these are good or bad, depends on his own stage of development, his own ethic and his own vision. He is able to direct his powers with intention at an object he wishes to obtain and apply them for intelligent action. Yet, it is also this Will which makes a Capricornian tough and unyielding in the attainment of his object. Looked at from the spiritual point of view, it is the spiritual drive of the Soul, the impulse to self-actualization, the striving for individuality which become active in Capricorn setting the creative power of the Will in motion.

The Awakening Of The Will

There are however other factors which cause the awakening of the Will. We have all experienced how in danger, in extraordinary emergencies or during a situation of pressure our own Will appears spontaneously and unexpectedly as a determining and liberating power. As soon as the Will has been freed from instinctual anxiety, it enables a person to grow beyond himself and to accomplish extraordinary achievements. For the Will to awaken a critical degree must be reached, a culmination of energy potential. Then the central energy of the Will emanating from the center of being awakens enabling individual action.

We have all said to ourselves at one time, "Yes, if it gets urgent, or if it's absolutely necessary, I'm capable of doing a lot." And it is in fact so; before the awakening of the Will, or the awakening to being, or before initiation, a person must undergo a crisis in which he has no other choice than to go forward. People who live thoughtlessly only for the day often need a blow of fate in order to come to their senses. Therefore, we should always adjust ourselves positively to every crisis because it will always bring an opportunity for growth.

The Crises Of Capricorn

All processes of self-becoming which end in a summit experience or in an initiation are accompanied by spiritual crises. These may have various characteristics and symptoms. Let us mention a few of them.

For example, when a person feels himself to be abandoned, alone and in profound need, then everything within him contracts; he stands there quite alone without vital human contact. Nothing else remains but "I am", his own life within his breast. This is a typical Capricorn experience which proceeds self-becoming. This "abandoned by all", this sojourn on a lonely height far-removed from the bustling activity of the world, this lonely existence must be experienced to the depths and is one of the most important experiences for the Capricornian, causing the necessary inner transformation. Esoterically this experience is called the "dark night of the Soul".

Loneliness makes us aware that we need each other, that we cannot live alone. But to take part in the warming powers of a communal life, we must become humble, we must descend from our throne and seek human contact. We shall recognize that we are not sacrificing anything, rather the opposite; we shall grow beyond ourselves, breaching the walls of the Ego, passing beyond Saturn, the Guardian of the Threshold, and entering into new consciousness. By humbling ourselves, by descending we also approach our own inner Self and sink our roots into the primal soil of all Being. From there new energies stream towards us, reviving, supporting and delighting us.

Certainly, whoever insists upon the rigid claims of his own Ego will shut himself off and harden himself in headstrong self-delusion, he will be threatened sooner or later by a breakdown. Then, in most cases, he realizes that in the end success gained in the world will not help him to overcome inner need and loneliness. Only when he has recognized the transience of material success and power after blows of fate, illnesses or loss and has turned decisively towards spiritual values, can he become happy again.

The Knee And Initiation

As we know the knee is ruled by Capricorn. That has a special meaning in this context. When the person born under Capricorn has learned to kneel in all humility and, with his knee on the rocky mountain summit, to dedicate his heart and his life to the Soul and to the service of humanity, then he can pass through the "gateway of initiation" and be entrusted with the secrets of life. Symbolically he can only pass through the gateway on his knees. As long as he stands arrogantly there where he has not yet earned the right to stand, he will never be able to make safe use of the energies of the Will and of life which flow through a powerful and self-confident personality and which may only be used for the benefit of the world. In accordance with the Seed Thought the Capricornian must be prepared to turn his back on the Light he has beheld, on the summit he has attained and on the height of his consciousness. Full of Love in his heart he must descend again to the Valley of Life as an example and leader to induce others to develop a responsible and dutiful personality and to lead them upwards to the summit of initiation.

Transformation In Motives

This whole process is concerned, first, with the right motivation for life, secondly, with the right use of the energies of the Will, and thirdly, with the application of the whole personality for ethical humanitarian aims, all egoistic aims having become meaningless. Yet, the Capricornian must accomplish this inner transformation of motives from the egoistic to the selflessly serving individual quite alone. He will then realize that the limitless loneliness of the consciousness which lives only for itself cuts him off from all living things and that he can only evolve further if he also works for others. Therefore, he must open himself to receive Universal and Divine Love, so that it may enable him to direct his Will with determination for the good of all humanity and to reject anything that opposes the laws of Love and of Life or which harms others. In so doing he will work in harmony with the laws of evolution. The blessing and abundance of all creation will then permeate him making him capable of genuine service for Mankind.

The Plan Of Evolution

We can see that the whole theme of Capricorn, of initiation, of self-becoming, unites us today to a special extent with energies which could be called the Will or Love or "Good Will". In reality it is that spiritual energy which flows out from our innermost Self, which is inherent in life and which gives an aim and purpose to the whole process of manifestation.

This life-giving energy helps us to overcome the forces of resignation induced by hardened states of consciousness which tempt us to see the negative side of everything. Moreover, outside in nature, covered at this time of year by the coldness of Winter, we can see life passing away. We are in danger of doubting whether life can go on, and yet we know from experience that life will blossom again in Spring. The Earth is already carrying within itself the seeds of life, just as we carry within ourselves knowledge and hope for the new life, even if it still appears cold around about us.

The Inner Light—Christ-Consciousness

In this way the joyous vision that everything brings about good develops within us. This inner Light has already been longed for at the Winter Solstice and finds symbolic expression in the birth of Christ.

At the time of the solstice we can cultivate a sphere of thought, above all through meditation, in the hope that faith and strength will grow in us and that we may consequently exert ourselves to a greater extent for the good and less for the bad around about us. Thus, we can persevere where almost nothing to be hoped for remains, still full of faith and in the enthusiastic fulfillment of duty.

Here and now we can all immediately give our active co-operation by purifying our sphere of thought and by inspiring others through our positive Will for life. The transforming power of Christ-consciousness lies in the recognition of the universal power of the heart. This demands a continuous control of the powers of the mind and of the feelings so that dark, discontented thoughts cannot spread. We should tune ourselves into that which rises, full of conviction, from our deepest heart, bringing more joy and happiness for us and for others. The Will, in combination with Love, is truly the energy which causes "a greater abundance" everywhere where it is properly applied, opening in us and around us inexhaustible springs of life, to which we wish today to open ourselves in meditation with gratitude and confidence.

Thus we begin the meditation.

Capricorn Meditation

1. Stage: Preparation

During the meditation we sit with a straight back. We close our eyes, but may open them occasionally if tensions arise. We rest our hands on our thighs and place our feet together. We achieve the greatest relaxation of the body by transferring our inner focus to the middle of our body. We let the upper part of our body turn slightly in a circular motion until we have the sensation of sitting at the focal point, at the Hara.

The breath also has a part to play in the preparation for the meditation. We breathe in and out four times. On exhaling we say, "Let go—Relax", then we hold our breath and think "Become one", on inhaling "Become new", we hold our breath, "Be yourself". We do this a few times.

2. Stage: Co-ordination

Co-ordination of the threefold personality, physical, emotional and mental with the Soul. For this exercise in integration we use after every stage the Sacred Word OM in order to shut out all disruptive vibrations.

a) The Physical Body
Our physical body is resting calmly and quietly on the chair, we are borne by the chair, secure in the house.

OM

b) The Emotional Body
We calm our emotions by imagining a sheet of blue water in which the Sun or the Moon is reflected.

OM

c) The Mental Body
Thoughts come and go. I remain quite calm listening into myself, looking at my thoughts, I do not let myself be distracted.

OM

Alignment With The Soul

We are inwardly secure, attuned to the good and the beautiful, quite prepared to come into contact with our innermost being. We imagine behind us a golden-white Sun. We gain contact with it by an impulse of the Will, by slipping into it with our consciousness. As a Soul we pour out with an inaudible OM Light, Love and power to our waiting personality.

3. Stage: Capricorn Visualization Exercise

I direct my attention to my brain. I look for the center in the middle of my head. I am quite alone within myself; quietness envelops me, I have plenty of time.

I allow the focal point to sink quite slowly within my head, between the jaws, through the neck, down to the upper breast. Here I let it rest and observe the place at the level of the heart at which I point when I say "I". Here I relax, yielding to the pulse of my heart.

Then I sink further within myself, lowering the focal point away from the heart to the waist and a little further down to the lower part of the body. There I find the focal point of the body. Down here I find peace and relaxation, creating the power for a new ascent. I am breathing quietly.

Then I ascend again. In my mind I imagine a steep mountain path in front of me which I climb slowly, step by step. The ascent is difficult and steep, yet I see the summit I long for before me. I clamber over bolders, obstacles, stones. I am getting nearer and nearer to the summit. Carefully and with stubborn energy I clamber up the last rock.

I have scarcely ascended it when I am struck by a blinding light; joy fills my breast. In majestic, divine solitude high, percipitous rockfaces tower above me on all sides, glaciers are lying bathed in blazing sunlight glistening in white light in the blue firmament. Up here in the clarity of the cold mountain air we find only sublime tranquility and endless peace. I allow myself to be penetrated by this blinding light. I breathe deeply; the air is clear and pure filling me with new life. I look beyond the mountain summits and then down into the valleys of surging life.

I think deeply about life. I feel a tugging of the heart. An intensive desire arises in me to descend and join humanity in love, to tell them of my summit experience and to show them the way so that they too may ascend. Then we meditate on the Seed Thought:

Lost am I in light supernal, yet on
that light I turn my back.

4. Stage: Group Endeavor

Then we raise our consciousness into our head and extend it lovingly to the people here in the room. We join with all those who approach the spiritual energies through meditation at the time of the Full Moon, forming a group unity on the mental plane receptive to the cosmic energies of the sign Capricorn.

We imagine how we all raise together a cup into the air in highly concentrated inner aspiration and readiness for the spiritual forces of Light and Love which flow into our receptive consciousness, symbolized by the cup. We slowly raise our hands.

We perceive a path of light stretching from our group to that source where the Love of God dwells, which is expressed on our planet through Christ. We feel ourselves to be enclosed within His Love and dedicate the group in the great process of transmission to the service of the world.

At the centre of all love I stand;
From that centre, I the Soul will outward move;
From that centre, I the one who serves will work.
May the love of the devine Self be shed abroad in my heart,
through my group and throughout the world.

We slowly lower our hands.

5. Stage: Transmission To Humanity

Now we turn to Mankind, allowing its needs, worries and burdens to flow into us, lifting them up to the Light of the Soul and praying for help from there. The living stream of the energy of Light, Love and creative Will flows through our being. We imagine to ourselves how these forces, like a net of light spread out over the whole planet, radiate out penetrating all areas of planetary life so that the spiritual forces can effect the events of the world, everywhere and at all times.

We transmit together the stream of energy through the Great Invocation to humanity.

From the point of Light . . .
(see page 234)

OM OM OM

Completion of the meditation (as before).

AQUARIUS

Notes • Thoughts on the Full Moon Meditation •
The symbol of Aquarius • The outer and the inner world •
Aquarius and the 7th ray • The twofold life of the disciple •
Overcoming of the duality and contrasts •
The spirit of Synthesis: universal consciousness •
Danger of Aquarius • Group formations •
The task of Aquarius • Saturn: Dweller on the Threshold •
The esoteric seed thought of Aquarius •
The planetary rulers Uranus, Saturn and Jupiter •
The polarity: Aquarius-Leo •
Opportunity—enlightenment—brotherhood •
Group consciousness—the key-note of Aquarius •
Woman's self-consciousness • The essence of love •
New thoughts and new ideals • Objectivity •
Summary • Aquarius-Meditation • Epilogue: the coming age •

AQUARIUS

AQUARIUS

Notes

Aquarius	11th sign of the Zodiac
Month	21 January–18 February
Cross	Fixed
Temperament	Air
Full Moon	Sun in Aquarius Moon in Leo
Houses	11th House/5th House Axis of Relationship
Problem Area	Friendship and Love
Planetary Ruler	exoterically Saturn and Uranus esoterically Jupiter
Seed Thought	"Water of Life am I, poured forth for thirsty men."

Thoughts On The Full Moon Meditation

Today at the Aquarius Full Moon we can obtain a further insight into the nature of meditation. Meditation is a process of absorption, intensification and concentration. It is submersion and inner contemplation in which we attempt to shut off external influences as much as possible in order to be able to concentrate on inner spheres, on inspiration and higher spiritual qualities.

Meditation is a process of awakening to life, a conscious experience of our own depths and of our actual Self. In so doing we penetrate to a region where religious pictures arise and where the roots of every living religion are to be found. For this reason there is no true meditation without a religious content.

Meditation is a good method of obtaining a better understanding of humanity and of its Self. It is concerned with essence and with what lies behind external appearance. It provides us with a real experience of what we recognize in theory and what we feel, think and desire. In short, meditation is work in itself. During meditation we learn to use our minds and understanding, not only outwardly, but inwardly as well so that we may prepare a way for ourselves to our true Self. Meditation is no passive, dreamlike state, but rather it awakens our highest spiritual abilities and erects a bridge between the outer and the inner world.

The Symbol of Aquarius ♒

The symbol of the sign Aquarius, on whose qualities we shall meditate today, shows two wave-shaped lines, one on top of the other. If we suppose that the upper one represents the spiritual and the bottom one the material principle, then we can see in the harmonious inter-reaction of these two forces a synthesis in the wave-like flow of the eternal alternating current of life. The inner and the outer world can be combined. In the Age of Pisces Man abandoned himself without trouble to the inner world, to mystical submersion; in the coming Age of Aquarius however we must learn to live and think in both worlds simultaneously. At the present time in particular we are faced with this problem. Today we are living in a world which is continuously drawing us away from the centre and to the periphery; it demands all our powers and all our concentration. The abundance of impressions, the agitation and rush are so great that we are continuously being diverted from our inner life. The incessant pull outwards, the unfulfilled desires for ever more possessions, the distraction through television, newspapers, magazines, store windows, advertisements and a thousand and one other superficialities demand our full attention. We must put a stop to all that when we set out seriously on the way inwards. We must direct our senses inwards for the undisturbed activation in inner experience of that source of spiritual power with which we can operate more casually, more calmly and more usefully in external life.

The Outer And The Inner World

In the Age of Aquarius the outer and the inner world must be brought together supplementing each other in a synthesis of rhythmic exchange. The meeting place of these two worlds is the consciousness of Man. The horoscope is also divided into an outer and an inner, an upper and a lower part. This corresponds to the prehistoric division into houses, which also has validity in meditation training, whereby the circle in the middle has a special significance. Man lives between the demands of the world and the requirements of his Soul. The one has as much reality as the other. If one of them is forgotten or neglected, then Man loses his centre of balance and must find his way back to this centre again through suffering and pain. However we all see ourselves faced with the problem—"In the midst of the burdens and struggles of modern existence how do we find the way to ourselves?" This concern in a material world which only chases after earthly things is indeed a great problem. It is no surprise that many daunted and give up the struggle and the striving. Many who search earnestly make external conditions responsible for their own failure and believe that if they could live freely in solitude without all the conditions and responsibilities, without the tiring obligations and professional demands, then they as well could lead a life of meditation. Such excuses are often based on self-deception.

In reality purely external, physical solitude and peace in no way remedy the basic problem of composing oneself inwardly. This has a much deeper cause. Normally, we take our inner turmoil, anxiety and distress with us into self-imposed solitude. We must therefore learn to find the way to our inner depths, even in the midst of the din of life around about us, so that a harmonious balance between the inner and the outer, the upper and the lower, may be found and that all our powers may be collected at the center. First however, we must find this center within ourselves, and to this end meditation is an aid.

Aquarius and the 7th Ray

According to Alice A. Bailey, the spirit of Aquarius is subject to the 7th Ray of ceremonial magic or of the cyclical and rhythmic order of life. Everything is rhythmic, in the life of nature as well as in the life of the Soul. Like the continuous alteration between Summer and Winter, day and night, waking and sleeping, every well-ordered life should run in a rhythmic alternation between tension and relaxation, concentration and expansion, meditation and practical activity, contemplation and service, inner and outer action, introversion and extroversion. However, this rhythm must never take on the rigidity of the cycles to which the natural phenomena are constrained, but should be adapted to the many different psychological and practical necessities of our complicated human existence. In Aquarius we are able to find our own individual life-rhythm. Our lives should be correctly organized and planned to be able to do this. In order to cope with the increased demands and the speed of life in our times, we cannot dispense with an intelligent division of the day. Every morning we should dedicate a little time to quiet contemplation or meditation; once a week at the end of six days we should allow a day for relaxation, and at least once, but preferably twice a year we should observe a period of withdrawal and solitude.

The Twofold Life Of The Disciple

In the Aquarius month in particular we can become clearly aware of these rhythms. The rhythmically alternating life of the disciple can also be understood in terms of the above-mentioned symbol of Aquarius, the twofold wave-like line. It is a dual situation, the solution of which lies in the conscious experience of these twofold rhythms simultaneously. With a part of our mind and of our perception we reflect on the spiritual life, and with the other part of our mental receptiveness we concentrate on life in its external form. This demands throughout the whole day a constant, meditative attitude, a simultaneous, profound anchorage in the foundation of our own Being and a toiling from this center outwards into life. Meditation is one of the most important ways of cultivating this state of consciousness and of maintaining it to a continuously improving degree. Correct meditation requires daily practice over a period of years because it is a condition which must only be built up slowly, bit by bit, stage by stage. Therefore, it is necessary to develop the right feeling for the period in Aquarius. Greater patience and perseverance, as well as the abandonment of haste and rush are important prerequisites.

So as I get a deeper insight into the qualities of the sign of Aquarius, we need to consider more closely the dualities to which we are all constantly exposed and the overcoming of which is one of the most important tasks of anyone born under Aquarius.

Overcoming Duality And Contrasts

The exoteric ruling planets of Aquarius are Saturn and, in more recent times, Uranus. Here is a duality from the outset. On the level of the mind this duality exists between the abstract ability of the mind, enlightened by intuition, and the concrete intellect which will only accept what can be proved scientifically and what is tangible and measureable. The waves of the sign Aquarius, lying one on top of the other, are a symbol for this as well. The upper wave indicates the spiritual, abstract mind corresponding to the planet Uranus; and the lower wave the concrete, Saturnian mind bound to material reality. Both modes of thought however should be united and mutually permeate each other. The concrete mind adjusted to material realization must be fertilisaed or illuminated by abstract and intuitive ideas. The unity of the two polarities however always occurs through the third additional factor, through the Spirit of Unity, of merging which is called esoterically the coming "Avatar of Synthesis", or through Jupiter, the esoteric Ruler of the sign Aquarius.

A further possibility for the overcoming of duality is that of detached observation or of conscious penetration of the Soul and personality. This ability presupposes a certain intelligence and power of discrimination, requiring these qualities so as to be one with the Soul or with the higher Self and to be able to observe oneself. It is good practice for us to distance ourselves from our Ego so far that we can hear ourselves talk and see ourselves act. Indispensible in this respect are detachment from the requirements of our "little Ego" and anchorage in the Soul so that we may always dwell in the position of the observer and are able to direct from that stand point and from that attitude the activity of the mind, of feeling and of action.

The most important exercise for detachment is the development of the ability to discriminate through objectivity and disidentification. We must learn to separate the essential from the inessential and to comprehend in a flash the momentary situation as it really is. We should catch hold of what is near, restricting ourselves to realities; we should give up illusions, perceive the possibilities for realization and engage ourselves completely. Then we shall no longer place so much value on so many of the trivialities which cost us time and energy, and we shall be able to engage our spirits with important things. A requisite for this however is the elucidation or objectivity of the feeling nature through no longer allowing ourselves to be discouraged by our feelings and through resisting with determination the urge to give up our high ideals on the grounds of self-satisfaction, material ambitions or self-pity. The main aim is therefore mental analysis, the discrimination between the real and the unreal. In this way we may recognize the deceptive nature of all our emotional reactions, their constantly alternating and self-contradicting manner of arousing often contrasting and ambivalent attitudes and reactions towards one and the same object.

The Spirit of Synthesis: Universal Consciousness

Beside the ability to discriminate, a sense of correct proportion is also important. It is connected with the "Spirit of Synthesis" from which a sense of humour develops; one no longer takes oneself so seriously. From the "position of self-observation" many reactions which one can now see in their true relationship to each other sometimes appear even ridiculous. Thus, one begins to laugh at oneself. This is particularly marked in German-speaking countries where during this month the Carneval is celebrated with all its joking and poking fun at oneself and others. Aquarius is indeed the 'joker', the actor and the clown. All these are the effects of the detachment process. By not taking ourselves so seriously any longer, we gain a greater perspective.

Dangers of Aquarius

But even here there is a danger! For if being detached goes too far the Aquarius either loses himself in utopias and ideas of world improvement which cannot be realized because they look too far into the future, or he no longer takes anything seriously and, placing himself above others, becomes an arrogant eccentric or crank who is incapable of anything. He becomes distrustful and exaggeratedly fastidious. Thus for example, he associates only with people whom he thinks are suitable for him and at the same stage of development as himself. In this way harmful prejudices can develop which cause him to reject brusquely all contact with lesser beings. His fellow man is no longer of value. His own Ego becomes swollen and in cold snobbery he passes into isolation, into an 'ivory tower'.

An Aquarian who ventures to such extremes feels that he is indeed so pure and holy that he becomes incapable of taking a proper interest in life. He is no longer interested in anything, only in his own pet ideas and in his own well-being. Everything else goes unnoticed or is haughtily rejected. He is bereft of experience, becoming distanced from life and engrossed in an imaginary world.

An Aquarian who isolates himself from others in self-conceit and self-righteousness—something which he does continuously—will without fail suffer psychological crises. He will come to recognize that he is impotent, that he can accomplish nothing alone and that he is cut off from the main stream of life. He must savour this impotency to the last dregs until such time as his pride and arbitrariness disappear. Only then will he be able to set out in search of others with whom he can find mutually useful solutions to existing problems. He must learn to unite and co-operate with others. With Aquarius it is love as well as his own distress which bring him back to his own center. In this the axis Leo-Aquarius plays a role in fetching him down from his ivory tower into which he has climbed. Love often arrives unexpectedly like a ray of sunlight softening the cool Aquarian heart.

Group Formations

As has already been said, the Aquarian who wants to evolve further must set out to find a group. He must seek those individuals who wish to work with him towards the same ideals. Thus, he becomes the leader of groups and organizations, of spiritual movements with worldwide influence. It is for this reason that we find under the Aquarian influence the group formations, the urge for union, for communes and combines, for the fusion of individual initiative and the team-work which are today so evident everywhere.

The Tasks Of Aquarius

The Aquarian has the ability to find original solutions to existing problems. He is the born inventor who shuns no difficulties when taking on complicated and involved tasks. He is capable of treading new paths and of introducing reforms which both relate to the inner sphere of life and at the same time also fulfill the demands of the external world. The true Aquarian always experiences the urge to abolish the abuses of the world. Indeed it can occur that his vision becomes darkened and that he only sees the abuses by which he becomes overwhelmed. This inherent urge to improve the world also often causes him to come up against the misunderstanding of the world around him, against rigid mental forms and against powerful ideologies and beliefs from the past, which are not only present in the world but also within him and which correspond to Saturn, the traditional Ruler of Aquarius. They get in the way of his spiritual endeavors. With them he must fight inner battles, learning to wrestle and cope if he wishes to dedicate himself and his life to new spiritual ideas and values.

Saturn—"Dweller on the Threshold"

Just as in Capricorn, Saturn also becomes in Aquarius the "Dweller on the Threshold" until such time as his ideals and visions correspond to reality and until he has matured to a secure understanding of reality. The Uranian, the Aquarian, who wishes to push through his new ideas must always wrestle with the stereotyped behavior of people who will only do something because it has always been done that way. At the same time, he must fight against his own tendency of having to hand a patent solution to all problems or of offering a definitive system into which everything suitable and unsuitable is squeezed simply because he imagined it that way. In his decidedly technical mind these systems may work; but they are usually suitable only for robots and scarcely for human beings possessing life and self-consciousness.

In all stagnated, crystallized and dogmatic habits of mind the Aquarian meets Saturn as Guardian of the Threshold. Only with the purest motives of true humanity, by placing his thoughts and ideas with a joyful heart at the service of all, can he overcome Saturn.

If on the other hand the Saturnian powers get the upper hand, he must pass through loneliness and depression; at least, as long as he encapsulates himself in his Ego and isolates himself from others. Only when he has unitied with others realizing projects communally with them, will defeats and failures no longer throw him off course or discourage him. He will then become a servant of humanity.

Aquarius is symbolized holding a jug of water. He pours the contents out onto humanity and thus becomes capable of "bringing a flood of unifying life into the hearts of Men which drives life onwards to unity and synthesis", as it is expressed in old texts.

The esoteric Seed Thought of Aquarius Runs:

"Water of life am I, poured forth for thirsty Men."

The Planetary Rulers Uranus, Saturn and Jupiter ♅ ♄ ♃

In Aquarius, Uranus and Saturn rule on the physical plane and Jupiter on the esoteric, in other words on the plane of consciousness. The influence of these Rulers can be defined simply: the Aquarian strives for friendly ties although at the same time maintaining his own personal originality. Through Uranus he shows open-mindedness towards everything new; through Saturn he is concentrated on himself. Here we have a dual situation, the opposition between old and new, between altruism and inner destiny. Only when he has united these two extremes within himself, will he be able to create with the aid of his finely developed Jupiterian sensory perception useful possibilities for solving the problems on hand; thus he sometimes becomes a successful inventor as well.

Aquarius is no scaler of summits like Capricorn; he is above things anyway from the outset. Uranus and Saturn as exoteric Rulers make sure that the Aquarian always remains on the borderline between the real and the possible. He would like to cross this border, to thrust forward into new dimensions. As soon as he has pushed through, Jupiter becomes effective, by whose influence he is able to see things in their correct perspective. His egocentric self-consciousness will expand into universal or group consciousness through which the final synthesis with the Cosmic Consciousness is attained in Pisces.

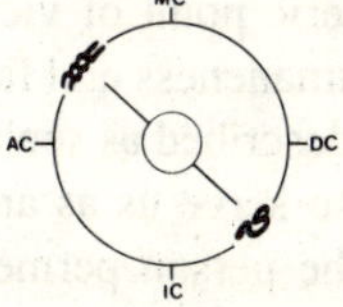

The Polarity Aquarius-Leo

The axis between Aquarius and Leo is an indication of this. In Leo self-consciousness is developed to its fullest extent; the individual awakens to his own identity; he concentrates his aim on attaining the goals of his personality. In the end he is so pushed into a corner by the progress of life that he becomes aware of the futility of his own self-interest. In Aquarius the individual recognizes that he can achieve nothing without others; he awakens to group-consciousness, to humanity, and recognizes his individual responsibilities to the group and to the individual human being. He begins "to lead his own life and to wear himself out in the service of humanity," as it is expressed esoterically. Aquarians are always very busy, usually with other people's affairs only. They frequently assume the responsibilities and duties of others and often they feel themselves to be of value, noble and good, when they are able to stand up for social justice.

Opportunity–Enlightenment–Brotherhood

These are the gifts which are bestowed on humanity during the month of Aquarius. In the house division of the horoscope Aquarius is situated in the upper house of consciousness and corresponds to the 11th House (cf. "Man And His World" by Bruno and Louise Huber). The Aquarian is, therefore, not so dependent on his own Ego, which is still being developed in Leo, the opposite sign. He has already passed beyond this stage. Thus, we are told that the Aquarian is group-conscious. This inner quality moves him to look after others, to stand up for them, to intervene from his loftier stand point with assistance and so to defend true, genuine, human values. Free of instinctual troubles, he can open himself to higher, ethical and ideal values. The intensive self-consciousness of Leo is expanded to awareness of the group in Aquarius. The individual becomes the universal. The solitary, distinctive human being becomes in his consciousness of unity the whole of humanity and yet maintains his individuality. He is no longer just an egocentric being, but in a certain sense he develops a planetary awareness of responsibility; from self-service he passes on to world-service and yet remains an individualized entity.

Group-Consciousness—The Key-Note Of Aquarius

This is an important idea, and we should therefore consider it more closely. From the esoteric point of view group-consciousness blossoms in Aquarius, resulting in humaneness and fairness towards the weak. Group-consciousness could also be described as social conscience. It is the key-note of the new Age and should also serve us as an inner basic theme in all our group work.

Although the person permeated with the spirit of Aquarius abandons his personal interests for the benefit of the whole, he maintains and preserves his own individuality. The belief is still very common—in accordance with the Age of Pisces—that we should abandon ourselves in a group and gather round a strong personality who is to be served submissively with true devotion.

This attitude is no longer valid today for we must all learn to accept self-responsibility. But this is something we can only do if we are true to ourselves and are able to remain so. Only then are we able to realize true group love. Genuine love can only be expressed when an individuals' self-consciousness is available as a focal point; and whoever feels himself to be recognized and acknowledged in his originality and uniqueness, is able to tolerate others as well and will realize genuine humanity. Thus rises the "Harmony of the Originals", as group-consciousness was once described.

Women's Self-Consciousness

It is also therefore particularly important today for a woman to develop greater self-consciousness. She must become aware that she represents ordering and preserving forces in the world. Only then can she stand up effectively for law and justice and assist in creating valid forms of life for all the people of this Earth, and thus contributing to the realization of Human Rights. For too long a woman based her self-consciousness on having a husband who loved her and with whom she lived in the legal bond of marriage, enjoying in this way social recognition. That is to say, she was only a valid human being when she had a husband; her self-consciousness was completely dependent on the love and recognition of the husband. If the man no longer loved her, he had the right to caste her aside; from then on she was just a nobody and was considered as second class by human society. All that has changed fundamentally in the present day; and women must be fully aware of this so that they can free themselves from the old attitude. This old attitude or conditioning is the "Dweller on the Threshold" confronting the woman of today. The confrontation with old, out-of-date forms of behavior is something which all women experience in common. It is not an isolated, but a human problem. It is no longer necessary for the woman of our modern times to make her self-consciousness dependent on the love or faithfulness of a husband. She now has the possibility of asserting herself in the world and of conquering a place for herself as a human being, whether in the field of work or in the family. This process is on the move throughout the world; everywhere it can be observed how women are becoming independent—which is also a reason for the frequent number of divorces.

But this alone is still not enough; it is really a question of the unity of all souls and of true Love or true humanity; it is a question of the balance between human being and human being. This is only possible through the third pole—through Love. Therefore, it is so important to know more about true Love. It is the Christ-Principle which should once again come alive in the hearts of men. As women are particularly suited to receiving the spirit of Christ in their hearts, it is probably their very special task to establish the same in the world.

In other words, the new self-consciousness which a woman must win for herself enables her more than ever before to become a true human being and to obtain true humanity because she is destined by nature to preserve life. This inner drive to preserve life at all costs requires the full capacity of our intelligence for finding and creating ever better opportunities so that life on our planet is not endangered. The natural protective and rearing function of a mother can today work in a new effective way. As her power increases through self-evolving self-consciousness, then she must stand up for true and genuine human values. And here the esoteric Ruler of Aquarius also comes into effect—Jupiter, who by means of a clear perspective brings all things into their correct relationship.

As women we must have the courage to advocate the vision of universal humanity. Where injustice and exploitation prevail, we must bravely stand up to them and fight for a just distribution and a just equalization. We should use our whole intelligence and skill to find the best solution—not only for our families and children but also for an ever increasing number of people.

The Essence Of Love

It is necessary to clarify our idea of Love and to adapt it to the new Age. Love is neither a sentimental stirring of feelings nor an emotion or a desire; Love is the working of a transcendental power and a transcendental process in us. Love does not begin in us, neither does it end in those we love. It has a cosmic source; it streams through us and at length continues on its way. The more we love, the more Love can arise on Earth. This clear Light of Love, as an energy of attraction, will wash away all sorrow and care which have arisen through ignorance and isolation and will offer joy as the key-note of the coming "New Age".

Today in the Aquarius meditation we can invoke the accurately evaluating, unifying spirit of the esoteric Ruler Jupiter so that disunity may be put aside and conflicts overcome, not only in ourselves but everywhere in the events of the world—so that people may continue more able not only to see what divides them, but that they may recognize the greatness of the unity of all things and may cultivate and promote that which binds and unifies. People who can clearly see the existence of need and who want to do something about it to bring about better conditions, can be found worldwide in many different organizations and groups, indeed in every field of human interest, whether in religion, in culture, education or in politics. It is these people who must be receptive to the inflow of enlightened wisdom and of that loving understanding which is possible today in a special way.

New Thoughts And New Ideals

From the outlook of the spirit of Aquarius we can deliberately concentrate in meditation on bringing new thoughts and ideals into the thinking of men, and thus to co-operate in the creation of a new and better world. However, this is only possible when we feel ourselves to be responsible for what happens in the world, when the "world conscience" has awoken in us or when objectivity has been attained. To arrive at this attitude of mind we must learn to renounce egoism, personal success and enrichment and to let extreme fairness rule in human relationships.

It requires the renunciation of the little personal Ego to be able to contemplate more objectively one's own Ego and one's fellow men from a superior stand point, from one's real Being, that is to say, as if from a distance, and to be able to acknowledge and judge them.

Objectivity

For this reason great value is placed in meditation training on the maintenance of objectivity so that one may better recognize what one is really like and may be receptive as well to the needs of others and to the problems of humanity. A certain amount of interest must already exist not only for human affairs but also for the alleviation of the need which exists all around us. The desire to serve and to help must be sincere, otherwise the creative Aquarius energies will have a disturbing effect on our small personal motives and will cause crises and difficulties.

When we stand up for these new forces, we are all too ready to believe that our activity is being criticized and falsely judged, or that our work and our efforts are not sufficiently valued, recognized or understood.

Discouragement and contempt are then the trials of Aquarius as well as of all those who advocate the realization of new values. We must therefore always defend ourselves against such feelings and inwardly arm ourselves, for they may undermine the edifying forces. Therefore, we must mutually protect and help each other by uniting in a common spirit and by increasing in strength through similarly directed thoughts and efforts, so that—in accordance with the spiritual image we have beheld—the best may be produced for all. Above all in meditation we produce together an area of solidarity and inner power. We should constantly remain in close contact with one another in order to stay firm and steadfast when out there in life we stand up for the spreading of genuine human values, of Good Will, compassionate understanding and justice.

Summary

In Aquarius therefore a constant alternation between Saturn and Uranus takes place. The discouragement and the anxieties come from Saturn, and the right opportunity and the illumination from Uranus. It is the path from "intellect to intuition" which brings about an amalgamation of these two principles. Saturn tests and has a mission of maturing to fulfill. When he has offered us an opportunity of growth, he normally puts us to the test, and we ourselves must decide whether we want to undertake a change and to take a step forward. Then we come under the law of Uranus. But usually we first have to overcome those fears which hamper the free expression of being of our inner Self. Only then will Saturn step to one side to make room for his big brother (or his sister) Uranus who allows the light of intuition and illumination to flash over the situation and wholly new ways to be beheld.

Through such enlightened thought and with the help of the esoteric Ruler Jupiter we can correctly assess and interpret events. Through the light of the present we can connect the old and the new, past and future. From this arises the usefulness of every meditation exercise; they enable us to let ourselves be led from within by the Light of the Soul. The practical success of this spiritual effort is dependent on the readiness to enlarge the inner Light and to use it for the establishment of human relations in the family, in the group, in the nation and in the world. As a group we can act in the Full Moon meditation as a receptive channel for these enlightening forces. Today we are especially called on to perform a great service for the benefit of humanity; in the Great Invocation we pray for the flowing in of Light, Love and power into the decisions of men. We can request and hope for the necessary illumination for all those who have to make decisions for humanity everywhere. Our individual enlightenment has nothing to do with this demand; it is as it were a side-product of this united group effort. It is a matter of selfless service. We ask for enlightenment and wise leadership for those who have to guide the destinies of races, nations and peoples. On their shoulders lies the responsibility of making wise decisions based on the world-wide understanding of the interests of international unity and on the establishment of just human relations. At the Aquarius Full Moon the realization of these motives is very much an important duty. We are called upon to support the forces of Light.

Thus we begin the meditation.

Aquarius Meditation

1. Stage: Preparation

We adopt a relaxed and comfortable attitude. Our backs are straight, our eyes closed. We may open them occasionally if tensions arise. We rest our hands on our thighs and place our feet together.

We achieve the greatest bodily relaxation by transferring our inner focal point to the middle of our body. We let the upper part of our body turn slightly in a circular motion until we have the sensation of sitting at the focal point, at the Hara.

Now we come to the breath which also belongs to the preparation for meditation. The peace, relaxation and composure which go together with the attitude of the body are deepened further by repeating five words for every four breaths. We know them already: "Let go, Relax, Become one, Become new, Be yourself." We exhale and think, "Let go, Relax"; we hold our breath and say "Become one"; when inhaling, which occurs automatically, we say "Become new", and when holding our breath "Be yourself". We do this a few times.

2. Stage: Alignment

Detachment and Self-perception *(Disidentification exercise according to Roberto Assagioli)*

a) The Physical Body
Today we achieve the co-ordination of the threefold personality by inwardly adopting the position of an observer and watching and experiencing ourselves as it were from the outside. We see ourselves sitting on our chair. The chair is borne by the house, the house by the Earth. We affirm, "I have a body. I look after it; I take care that it is always in good health; but it is not myself. I have a body, I have hands, feet, arms, but I am not my body."

b) The Emotional Body
Then I concentrate on my feelings and sensations. I have various feelings: joy, happiness, satisfaction, but also annoyance, anger and impatience. All these feelings belong to Man. They are uncountable; they contradict each other and change constantly. Feelings are like a stream flowing through me. I look at them but do not hold on to them if I do not want to. I know that I always remain myself. I experience sensations, but I am not my sensations. I have wishes, but I am not my wishes—they are not my Self.

OM

c) The Mental Body

Now I concentrate on the thoughts in my head. Thoughts come and go, but I remain. I have a mind, but I am not my mind. It is active, concentrated or undisciplined, yet it may be instructed. It is an organ of knowledge not only with respect to the external world but to the inner as well, but it is not my Self. I have thoughts, but I am not my thoughts.

OM

Alignment With The Soul

After this dissociation or differentiation of the Ego from its physical, emotional and mental tools or captivity we are able to penetrate to that region in which our innermost being resides, the Self or the Soul.

With a dynamic act of will we identify ourselves with the Soul. We perceive a shining bright Sun behind us. As a Soul we silently sing OM and pour out Light, Love and compassion onto the expectant, integrated personality. Thus the personality is strengthened in service.

3. Stage: Aquarius Visualization Exercise

Then we extend this shining white Light to our neighbours here in the circle joining with the Light of the whole group. A bell of Light is formed which extends upwards to the highest point in the center. We hold this bell of light in our consciousness and at the same time imagine it opening very slowly from the upper centers; a delicate tone is sounded and a radiant golden light pours out of the opening, flowing down to us and penetrating our threefold personality. Then we meditate on the Seed Thought of Aquarius:

"Water of life am I, poured forth for
thirsty men".

I feel this revitalizing substance invigorating me and giving me new impulses, inspiration and power. I feel it flowing through me and uniting me with everything that lives. I am reborn as it were into a new dimension where I am one with everything that exists. This experience fills me with great joy. I feel secure, supported by the unity of all life. Life penetrates all things, unites all things, yet I myself remain unchanged; I am not extinguished through the experience of unity. I can perceive clearly this unity, this first cause of all Being. My consciousness unfolds further and further becoming permeable to the power of Universal Love which I pour out to all humanity.

Mantram Of Unity

The sons of men are one, and I am one with them.
I seek to love, not hate;
I seek to serve and not exact due service;
I seek to heal, not hurt.

4. Stage: Transmission to humanity

Then we turn to humanity and allow this living stream of the energy of Light, Love and creative Will to pour through us into the consciousness of humanity and to expand there. In so doing we imagine how these powers are caught up by numberless points of light spreading themselves out like a net of light over our whole planet; how they radiate penetrating all areas of our planetary life so that these spiritual forces may be at work everywhere and at all times in the events of the world.

Together we transmit the energy stream to humanity through the Great Invocation.

From the point of Light . . .
(see page 234)

OM OM OM

Completion Of The Meditation

We open our eyes, breathe in and out deeply once, moving our head, our neck, our shoulders, our feet, our hands. Then we extend to each other our hands, look into each other's eyes and bow before each other.

EPILOGUE

The Coming Age

Aquarius is of the greatest significance for our present time. It is the sign of the coming Age into which the First Point of Aries is moving in the World horoscope. Its influence increases in significance and in additional effectiveness with every decade. Together with the three new planets Aquarius is responsible for the changes which are now being felt in all the affairs of human life. As it is an Air sign it can make its influence penetrate everywhere and become effective there. Many have still not perceived this influence at all, in spite of which these forces are penetrating all forms of manifestation and are having a far more far-reaching effect than the more concrete events which catch the eye. They are subjective, powerful streams of energy which are causing changes in our planetary life and in all the realms of nature.

The increased inflow of the Aquarius quality is having a twofold effect: first, the dismantling and diminishing of the dividing walls of egoism which express themselves in Man as selfishness and in peoples as nationalism; secondly, the pouring out of a powerful flood of unifying life into the hearts of men uniting them with new bonds and with a brotherhood of Mankind which will overcome all racial and national differences and will bring the life of Man to synthesis and unity.

PISCES

Notes • The sign Pisces • Invocation, Evocation and prayer • The longing of Piscians • The symbol of Pisces • The path of the soul—the return • Sacrifice and death • Polarity Pisces–Virgo • The germ of the self-unfoldment • The capacity for sympathetic understanding • The mystical disposition—the experience of duality • Life and death • The planetary ruler • Transformation and birth of the ego • The esoteric seed thought of Pisces • The redeeming function • In the new age: joy instead of suffering • Pisces—Meditation • The seed thoughts and the ascendant-signs • The Great Invocation •

PISCES

PISCES

Notes

Pisces	12th sign of the Zodiac
Month	19 February–21 March
Cross	Mutable
Temperament	Water
Full Moon	Sun in Pisces Moon in Virgo
Houses	12th House/6th House Axis of Existence
Problem Area	Opposition of spiritual and physical existence.
Planetary Rulers	exoterically Jupiter and Neptune esoterically Pluto
Seed Thought	"I leave the Father's home and turning back I save."

The Sign Pisces

The sign Pisces is the mutable Water sign of the Zodiac. For this reason the feelings are very prominent. The person born under Pisces is a feeling type. He understands all the nuances of feeling and of inner emotions of the most subtle kind; which makes him very sensitive. It is the sign of devotion—Pisces people can identify with what they love. They often lose themselves in this self-abandoning love and will do everything in almost abject self-sacrifice for the loved one. This ability of the sign Pisces can help us today at the Pisces Full Moon to identify with our innermost Being. It is this ability for devotion which leads us on to become one and which joins us with the divine source from which we once originated. It is a projecting force which gives us a connecting path to our inner Being and thereby access to the transcendental world. This is a special process for coming into contact with that realm which we seek and which we also need in order to perform effective tasks in the world. This brings us into contact with a purpose for existence which is greater than our present one. Even the slightest hint of this readiness for devotion counts as a contribution to the great plan of evolution which is drawing all life on this planet towards perfection. Through genuine devotion to a greater purpose our small personal Will is united with the Divine Will; we are borne by the idealizing and inspiring power of our inner vision which bestows wings on us.

Invocation, Evocation And Prayer

In order to make contact now with these spiritual sources of life pouring out of our deepest Being, we meditate and recite at the conclusion of each meditation the "Great Invocation". Invocation is quite simply the appeal to higher energies and qualities. When we have a deeper understanding of the creative effect of invocation and evocation, we shall be able to achieve better results. We can be sure that an answer may be expected to every appeal. The answer is the evocation, the reaction, which we ourselves have called forth. If we imagine that the signs of the Zodiac are the qualities and substances of a living entity then we call upon these as it were in our sign—meditation expecting that they will reveal themselves to us and will answer us.

Since time immemorial Man has tried to approach higher energies or powers in prayer. A great mystic once said, "Prayer is the cry of the heart which recognizes powers that are greater than its own." Whenever someone gets into need, he starts to pray. He turns to an almighty divinity from whom he expects help. Man had already found refuge in prayer before the dawn of history even began. Here I think of the ape who forgot to eat up his banana at the setting of the Sun because he was lost in deep contemplation. Later human beings became more and more aware that they were surrounded by powers which they could contact and from which they could expect help. At first they called upon these powers by means of sacrifices and subjection in involved rituals and supplications, as is still the case today among primitive peoples. Later religious ceremonies arose, devotion and divine service. There will always be some form of prayer or refuge seeking. The science of invocation and evocation, the so-called Mantra-Yoga, is the most modern form of expression of this inner necessity to co-operate with higher powers. All forms of meditation and all opportunities of seeking contact with the subtler, spiritual world follow the laws of invocation and meditation. It is a demand which finds a ready supply, or as it is expressed in the Bible, "I shall meet you half way." That is the inner event of the sign Pisces.

The Longing Of Piscians

In the sign Pisces we long for an end, for peace and quiet, for a country that "speaks our language", for a divine home. For this reason the death wish occasionally arises here. At the same time however the budding forces of new life and of a new beginning are latent in Pisces. It is the sign of the return to the Father's home from which we once set forth, from which we began our journey through life. It is the sign in which death and life, beginning and end secretly meet and in which the old unites with the new. When the old has passed away or has been extinguished, we look around for something new which will revive us again and allow us to advance further. Advancement also corresponds to the feet which are under the rulership of Pisces!

The esoteric Seed Thought of Pisces Runs:

I leave the Father's home and turning back I save.

In this Seed Thought something is said about the double effect of Pisces. We set forth leaving the elevated place of the Soul, we incarnate in the physical body becoming its prisoner and longing all our life to return to the freedom and liberty of spiritual existence.

The Symbol Of Pisces ♓

Pisces belongs to the dual signs. Its symbol consists of two fishes or scales joined together by a band. One scale represents the Soul, the other the personality or form of Man. The two scales are bound together during the period of manifestation by a horizontal line—the thread of life or Sutratma. Beginning and end, life and death, Man and Cosmos meet here. One of the key-words of Pisces is servitude or imprisonment. In the first part of the evolutionary cycle when the Soul is incarnating, it becomes the prisoner of matter. In the second half following inner conversion when Man is already on his way back to his Father's home, the personality becomes the prisoner of the Soul.

The Path Of The Soul—The Return

A further key-word for Pisces is renunciation or dissociation. This key-word also has double meaning. First the Soul renounces the security of its own home which is symbolized by the word "my Father's home"; it descends into the ocean of matter, into darkness; it identifies itself with this form and forgets its true divine origin. Only through suffering and pain does it awaken again to its true consciousness and turns anew to spiritual things.

We realize that material security, success, recognition and possessions cannot help us a great deal because everything terrestrial is transcient. We realize the futility of everything material because we can take nothing with us when death knocks at the door. Thus in Scorpio, which is also a Water sign, the great inner conversion occurs and in Pisces we return home again. On the way we meet many others whom we tell of our own experience showing them the enthusiasm, the dedication, the renunciation and the dissociation from the captivity of matter so that they as well may set out on the return journey.

Sacrifice And Death

The third key-word is "sacrifice and death". This is described in "Esoteric Astrology" (pages 116–117) by Alice A. Bailey as follows:

> The Lords of the Will and Sacrifice come down into manifestation, sacrificing their high position and opportunities upon the higher planes of manifestation in order to redeem matter and raise the lives by which it is informed (the lower Creative Hierarchies) to the status of Themselves in so far as They constitute the fourth Creative Hierarchy. This is the subjective purpose, underlying the sacrifice of these divine Lives Who are ourselves essentially, Who are qualified by knowledge, love and will, and animate by ceaseless persevering devotion. They seek to bring about the death of the form in its occult significance and the consequent release of the indwelling lives into a higher state of consciousness. Of this process, all the world Saviors—past, present and to come—are manifested symbols and the eternal guarantees. It is in such recognitions as those that the mainspring of the life of service must be sought. People born in this sign are frequently to be found serving the race and ministering to its needs upon some level of consciousness. Thus they are prepared for the final sacrifice in Pisces which "absorbs them back into their originating Motive," as the Old Commentary expresses it.

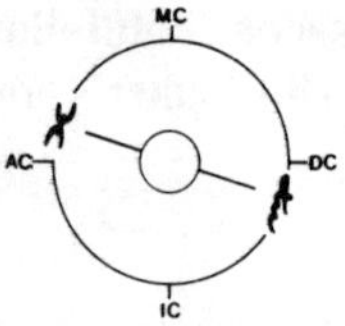

The Polarity Pisces–Virgo

As we know, in the sign Virgo we must work and earn our daily bread and keep everything in order so that life is secure. In Pisces on the other hand we do not want to know anything about all that. We look for consciousness freed from all earthly needs. When the needs of existence have been stilled and the accomplishment of our daily duties is no longer our only guiding principle, then we open our consciousness to new dimensions. We are open to Being, to the transcendental Whole. The Universal Consciousness arises to the light of day, whose power to transform leaves all static limitations behind, corresponding as it does to the dynamic of self-evolving life.

In Pisces we can relax for once taking it easy and dropping everything which distresses us. Sometimes we should accept an illness which comes to us as an opportunity to relax and to find our way back to ourselves. Thus the healing powers of the Soul are set free again. Many people in this month experience the desire to get up and go away as they long for the far-away, for peace and quiet and wish above all to leave behind them everything that oppresses them. They are escaping from the responsibilities of daily life. That is the polar tension between Pisces and Virgo—the axis of existence.

In the Pisces month we are able to learn that there is no security in the world, something for example which Virgo is always seeking, and that security lies in insecurity, or to express it better, in the pure condition of continuous consciousness. However, consciousness is only continuous when it is constantly in movement, never stopping still but always in movement, in flux and journeying onwards.

The Germ Of Self-Unfoldment

In a secret way the beginnings of life lie in the sign Pisces where the germ or Ego-experience begins to form although not yet visible. Just as outside in nature the buds are still closed although the power of life is already pulsating within them, so similarly both these forces are at work in Pisces. The preparation for that which is to come reposes in Pisces; here the spiritual is a challenge and an ideal for the future, although not yet present reality. The higher world exists usually only in the imagination. Therefore many Pisces people very often live in a visionary dream-world which hardly corresponds to reality.

The Capacity For Sympathetic Understanding

At the root of the nature of a person born under Pisces no hardness or extreme desire to impose the Ego can be found whatsoever. They are much rather inspired by a willingness to help, compassion and an intuitive capacity to understand sympathetically the nature of other people. This can be hardly praised enough in our contemporary achievement-oriented society; and herein lies the danger of the abuse of this sensitivity. Such people are often suppressed and remain more or less in the background. They are often little suited to carrying on the struggle for existence.

Pisces people always seek harmony in closer relationships because they find every argument, every conflict and the compulsion to succeed unpleasant. A feeling of being misunderstood often predominates and can be the cause of depressive moods. Nowhere does he feel at home; he longs for "a land that speaks his language", for people who understand him deeply. There is frequently an abyss between his feeling and rational world and his immediate or distant environment. Whatever he considers to be his most sacred feelings and ideals are abused by his fellowmen through misunderstanding or dispragement. At times he suffers badly from this. The cause of this suffering is his idealistic view of the world whose realization is difficult if not even impossible—and his environment is continuously holding it painfully before his eyes.

The Mystical Disposition—The Experience Of Duality

The mystical disposition of the Piscean causes him to seek the highest in all things; he would like to extinguish sober reality and give it another meaning. On the one hand he looks for deviant things which often make a great idealist and mystic of him, and on the other hand he is disposed to reinterpret life giving reality another meaning. If he aspires too high, then this attitude may become a living lie; his life does not agree with his ideas. Harnessed to the great opposition between spirit and matter, he can only find with difficulty a way of uniting them. This is the experience of duality which causes psychological problems and spiritual crises not only in the sign Pisces but in all other mutable signs as well. The symbol of the two fishes standing upright represents visually this duality. This is the opposition between Soul and personality which manifests itself as duality. It is also the "two Souls in my breast" which is so often sung and which represents two parts of being.

One part of the Piscean wants to surrender to everything, to merge with everything because everything means for him the Great Whole. It is the longing of the mystic to merge into the Cosmic Consciousness. He hardly fears losing himself because he senses inwardly that he will find himself again in the Great Whole. The other part however wants to remain itself. It wants to experience individuality in its highest form, but fears the total isolation and the loneliness which each individual consciousness must learn to bear.

Life And Death

In the sign Pisces the destructive forces of death often struggle for predominance with the new urge for manifestation. As this watery Neptunian sign easily drives Pisceans into a condition of boundlessness, the danger exists that the forces of dissolution, which Freud called the "death drives", will in fact get the upper hand. When the drives have become bound by this death wish, a struggle breaks out for the maintenance of life. If the outcome is positive the old is overcome and extinguished so that the new is brought to life. Essentially, it is a question of overcoming the abyss which lies between life and death. We can only achieve this through the unalterable will to live, otherwise we are drawn into the void and lose that genuine sense of reality which belongs to a healthy life.

Everything therefore depends on our own Will to live which must be strong enough to penetrate our becoming new. In this month we will all struggle in some way or other for life, whether it is physically because we are ill, or emotionally when we are discouraged and disillusioned, or mentally when we can only see the negative side of things and are in danger of falling into a depression. We must defend ourselves against all these degrading forces by affirming life as it is and by endeavoring to make the best of everything.

The Planetary Ruler ♃ ♆ ♇

In respect of this consideration of life and death, it is interesting that Jupiter is the exoteric and Pluto the esoteric Ruler of the sign Pisces. Jupiter, who transmits the energy of the Second Ray of Love and Wisdom, joins the two fishes, which represent Soul and form, bringing them into a functional relationship with one another. Through this magnetic power new life arises.

Pluto on the other hand transmits the energy of the First Ray of Will and power; it is concerned with the capacity for resignation and the formation of the Will which were mentioned at the beginning. The planet Pluto has a relationship to death, although not necessarily in the physical sense. It frequently indicates the death of old states and cycles which come and go. Pluto also represents the connection with physical death which turns everything into deep sleep extinguishing every living thing so that the new may arise and a new cycle of manifestation or of the expression of life can begin. We must consent to this renewing by collecting will-power for life into our own centers of Being by offering our purified Ego-centers for the service of the world. This will happen in the sign Aries.

In the symbol Pisces a ribbon joins the two characteristics of life. This ribbon is the center; it is the Ego and represents symbolically the seat of the true Self which has a comprehending relationship to the inner as well as to the outer world. It is the deepest center of Being which unites everything within itself, the individual as well as the Universal Consciousness. A similar symbol is indeed the Cross which has received such a deep significance through Christ in the Age of Pisces. The center of the Cross as the point of consciousness unites the inner and the outer, what is above and what is below. In order to achieve true self-consciousness the Piscean should neither lose himself in boundless nothing nor isolate himself in a too subtle Ego-feeling, but rather he must find the center which connects him to the transcendental world.

Transformation And Birth Of The Ego

Thus in Pisces a genuine transformation of one's own Ego takes place. This transformation is similar to the experience of dying and being born again in Scorpio. But it takes place in our own Self, in quiet and solitude, far from the noisy bustle of the world. The transformation and the becoming new come as it were like "the thief in the night on soft soles"—often without being noticed. A new dimension bursts into one's consciousness—as in nature the day awakens after a longing full of promise was felt in the twilight. The quality of Pisces is similar to this twilight. We pass beyond what previously appeared so important to the world-orientated Self. We become receptive to higher, spiritual impressions once night or sleep has extinguished all previous impressions. We again become humble, almost as devout as a child, innocent, resigning to something higher. We adjust ourselves to the Great Whole and feel ourselves to be secure because we have renounced ourselves and have overcome personal demands.

This occurs with relative ease in Pisces and in the Pisces month, for most drives are now at peace—but only for a short while before new life awakens again rushing on over us and before worldly things once again demand our attention. In this period of peace we arrive at the reality of our own Self—in a higher sense, at a stage of contemplation. In this "period of peace between two activities" the magnetic field is conceived which carries us outwards or inwards to the innermost part of our Being, to the unity with the WHOLE. Within this inner nucleus of existence is the Being from which all life proceeds and to which it returns. It is the Great Life of the ONE in whom we live, breathe and have our Being. The sign Pisces strives for this universal consciousness. It feels itself to be uplifted there.

In order to attain the vibrational field of the ONE LIFE, we need the metamorphic force of the esoteric Ruler Pluto. He destroys the tie which chains us to matter. Pluto leads directly to the innermost center of existence and brings everything out from the lower regions to the surface to destroy it there. This can be considered as a type of psychoanalysis.

As has already been mentioned Pluto is concerned with death, destruction of form and transformation. If in Pisces we can correctly understand death and dying and can accept them, then herein lies at the same time the overcoming of our little Ego which connect us to this world. This leads us to a perception of a greater life and a deeper existence within ourselves. We have all experienced this before: when we transported ourselves into the realm of the impossible renouncing our little Egos, we felt within that we had been caught up by a higher order and by a deeper meaning; and at the same time the inexplicable which occurred to us returned to its place and troubled us no more. This is felt by the Piscean who allows himself to sink into his own depths, caught up from somewhere else and enthused by a love and a warmth which are not of this world, which however receive him and hide him in his abandonment. The unifying powers of our own Self, the experience of a greater life and being, the unity of all souls make Pisceans vulnerable. In this experience, which exceeds death, paradox and the abandonment of the world, lie sources of a new life and a new beginning in the sense, "Behold, I make all things new." These words are announced to us promisingly by Christ who is considered the Redeemer of the world and who has an essential connection with the sign Pisces.

The esoteric Seed Thought of Pisces runs:

I leave the Father's home and
turning back I save.

The Redeeming Function

H. P. Blavatsky has clearly indicated the redeeming function of Pisces (Vol. 1, page 717), that constellation shines as a symbol of all past, present and future Spiritual Saviors who dispense light and dispel mental darkness."

It is a good idea to form a clear picture of the role of a Redeemer, because the selfishness and comfortableness of the average man have created a false conception of the existence and function of a Redeemer. Thus in the Christian Age in particular the belief has arisen that redemption may be attained through the vicarious sacrifice of one who has borne the burden of the sins of others. Many think that it is merely necessary to believe in the Redeemer showing personal devotion to him and to pray to him in order to achieve in this way redemption and to be accepted into paradise. This is a naive idea of the true nature of the Redeemer.

Redemption means above all release from the servitude of life on the three lowest planes, freedom from the wheel of rebirth. Redemption means detachment from material desires and wishes, and consequently transformation of the personality. Redemption therefore demands personal effort and active co-operation of each individual person. There are various ways and types of inner release.

In The New Age: Joy Instead Of Suffering

In the new Age the emphasis with regard to redemption will not lie in sacrifice and suffering as in the past, but in joy, a fact which is expressed in the following inspiring words," . . . A new form of redemption will arise . . . The cup of suffering and the agony of the Cross are nearing their end. Joy and strength will take their place. Instead of suffering we shall experience joy which will turn into happiness and will lead finally to blessedness. We shall have the power which knows nothing else but victory." This redeeming mission of Pisces is clearly expressed in the Seed Thought and will bring us release from the fear of death; for death is no more than the change into another state of consciousness in which new life presses towards unfoldment.

Thus we begin the meditation.

Pisces Meditation

1. Stage: Preparation

We are sitting with a straight back. Our eyes are closed, but we may open them occasionally if tensions arise. We rest our hands on our thighs, but may also open them like two bowls. We place our feet together.

We achieve the greatest bodily relaxation by transferring our inner focus point to the middle of our bodies. We let the upper part of our body turn in a circular motion, until we have the sensation of sitting at the focal point, at the Hara. The breath also has a part to play in the preparation for the meditation. We inhale four times and say on exhaling, "Let go—Relax", we hold our breath, "Become one", we inhale, "Become new", we hold our breath, "Be yourself". We do this a few times.

2. Stage: Alignment of the Threefold Personality

For co-ordination or identification we use the sacred word OM after each of these three stages in order to shut out all disruptive influences by applying magical, creative power.

First the physical body: we are sitting on the chair and are borne by the chair, by the Earth, by our planet; we are secure and safe in the house. We become quite heavy transferring our weight to our lower body and pumping some air in. Our backs are upright and our jaws relaxed. I allow all my muscles to relax without holding on to anything, I feel in to my forehead keeping it loose and relaxed. My forehead becomes smooth, my face friendly, my tongue lies in my lower jaw, my breath passes freely and evenly through my nose, "I am breath". We dedicate our physical bodies to the service of the Soul.

OM

The emotional body is calmed by imagining a sheet of blue water which becomes ever calmer; the waves are smoothed out. The light of the Sun or of the Moon plays on the waters. We feel love for all humanity and dedicate our emotional body to the service of humanity.

OM

The mental body: we free our Egos from our thoughts. Thoughts come and go. We watch them calmly relaxing and not allowing ourselves to be disturbed. We are free. We dedicate our thoughts to the good of all Mankind, to unfoldment and to the maintenance of life, to the Divine Plan for human evolution.

OM

Alignment With The Soul

We now allow our focal point to glide quite slowly down within our heads, (as a snail crawls), between our jaws, through our necks until it reaches our breast. Here we let it rest. Slowly our attention, our focal point, glides down further from our upper breast, to the middle of our body behind the breast bone, to the level of the heart—to the place to which I point when I say "I". Here we rest. Here I relax with my whole existence and Being. I allow the OM to sound silently within me and like the rolling of waves the tone carries everything with it outwards: everything burdensome, all worries, troubles and anxieties are washed away by the purifying, sacred TONE vibrating within me.

Then a point of the deepest calmness and peace arises within me; it spreads like a vacuum which surrounds me like a protecting envelope.

3. Stage: Pisces Visualization Exercise

I have plenty of time, endless time. Nothing is pushing me. I give myself up completely to this soundless stillness which connects me with eternity. I listen expectantly with all my senses into the stillness, alert to that which will make itself known and grow within me.

Suddenly I see before me a long corridor, narrow and dark. In the distance a light is shining, I recognize a bright form which beckons me. I am drawn towards it as if by magnetism. I let everything go and walk slowly along the corridor towards the form. It comes towards me calling my name, which touches me personally, echoing after me. We meet each other and look into each other's eyes with deep recognition.

Then it lays its arm upon my shoulders and says, "You have reached your goal. Come, follow me." Together we walk into the Greater Light.

We meditate on the Seed Thought:

I leave the Father's Home and turning back I save.

4. Stage: Group Endeavor

We extend our consciousness out over our surroundings and join with the people around us and with all those who approach the spiritual energies at Full Moon in meditation. We form a group unity on the mental plane receptive to the cosmic energies which are now available. We behold a path of light stretching from humanity to that source where the Love of God dwells, which is expressed on our planet through Christ. We feel ourselves to be enclosed within this love and dedicate the group to the service of the world.

We imagine how we all raise together a cup into the air in a highly concentrated inner aspiration, in an appeal to the spiritual powers of Light and Love which flow into our receptive consciousness—symbolically into the raised cup. We raise our hands very slowly:

Oh, Thou in whom we live, breathe and have our
being, the power which makes all things new,
turn the fate of Men to better things,
everywhere move the hearts of Men so that they
may open themselves to the spirit of love and
brotherhood and mutual responsibility.
May the Will for Good be the motive of all deeds
and may it establish once again the reign of
peace on Earth.
May the love of the divine Self be shed abroad in our heart,
through our group and throughout the world."

Stage: Transmission To Humanity

We slowly lower our hands and turn to humanity. We let this living stream of the energy of Light, Love and creative Will flow through us into the consciousness of Mankind and to spread itself.

We transmit the stream of energy together to Mankind through the Great Invocation.

From the point of Light . . .
(see page 234)

OM OM OM

Completion Of The Meditation

We open our eyes inhaling and exhaling once deeply. We move our head, our neck, our shoulders, our feet, our hands. Then we extend to each other our hands, look into each other's eyes and bow before each other.

THE SEED THOUGHTS AND THE ASCENDANT SIGNS

The knowledge transmitted in this book about the spiritual backgrounds of the twelve signs of the Zodiac is particularly important for those who have their Ascendant in the corresponding sign. The Ascendant among other things represents a transcendental dimension from which we come and to which we shall return. The esoteric Seed Thought gives us an indication of how we can develop the spiritual quality of our Ascendant sign. We have introduced them here once again in order.

Seed Thoughts Of Each Sign Of The Zodiac

Aries.	I come forth and from the plane of mind I rule.
Taurus.	I see, and when the Eye is opened, all is illumined.
Gemini.	I recognize my other Self and in the waning of that Self I grow and glow.
Cancer.	I build a lighted house and therein dwell.
Leo.	I am That and That am I.
Virgo.	I am the Mother and the Child, I God, I matter am.
Libra.	I choose the way that leads between the two great lines of force.
Scorpio.	Warrior I am, and from the battle I emerge triumphant.
Sagittarius.	I see the goal. I reach the goal and see another.
Capricorn.	Lost am I in light supernal, yet on that light I turn my back.
Aquarius.	Water of Life am I, poured forth for thirsty men.
Pisces.	I leave the Father's Home and turning back I save.

THE GREAT INVOCATION

From the point of Light
within the Mind of God
Let Light stream forth into
the minds of men.
Let Light descend on Earth.

From the point of Love
within the Heart of God
Let love stream forth into
the hearts of men.
May Christ return to Earth.

From the center where the
Will of God is known
Let purpose guide the little
wills of men—
The purpose which the
Masters know and serve.

From the center which we
call the race of men
Let the Plan of Love and
Light work out.
And may it seal the door
where evil dwells.

Let Light and Love and
Power restore the Plan
on Earth.

This invocation does not belong to any person or group, but to the whole of humanity.

The beauty and strength of this Invocation lies in its simplicity, and in its expression of certain central truths which all men, innately and normally, accept—the truth of the existence of a basic Intelligence to Whom we vaguely give the name God; the truth that behind all outer seeming, the motivating power of the universe is Love; the truth that a great Individuality came to Earth, called by Christians, the Christ, and embodied that Love so that we could understand; the truth that both love and intelligence are effects of what is called the Will of God; and finally the self-evident truth that only through *humanity* itself can the Divine Plan work out."

Alice A. Bailey

BIBLIOGRAPHY

Assagioli, Roberto. *Psychosynthesis—a Manuel of Principle and Techniques*. New York: Viking Press, Inc., 1971.

Bailey, Alice A. *The Externalization of the Hierarchy*. New York: Lucis Publishing Company, 1951. London: Lucis Press Ltd., 1951.

——— *Cosmic Fire*. New York: Lucis Publishing Company, 1951. London: Lucis Press Ltd., 1951.

——— *White Magic*. New York: Lucis Publishing Company, 1951. London: Lucis Press Ltd., 1951.

——— *Esoteric Astrology* (A Treatise on the Seven Rays III). New York: Lucis Publishing Company, 1951, London: Lucis Press Ltd., 1951.

Blavatsky, H. P. *The Secret Doctrine*. Adyar, India: The Theosophical Publishing House, 1938.

Bhagavad-gita. New York, 1952.

Jung, Carl G. *Collected Works Part II*. New York: Aion, 1959.

Ptolemaei, Claudij. *Tetrabiblos, De Praedictionibus Astronimicis*, Philippo Melanthone, Basileae, Per 10 annem Oporinum.

Ptolemy, Claudii. *Ptolemaei Tetrabiblos*. Leipzig, Germany: Ed. F. Boll and E. Boer, 1940.

Rudhyar, Dane. *The Astrology of Personality*. New York: Lucis Publishing Company, 1936.

Eastcot, Michael J. *The Silent Path*. York Beach, Maine: Samuel Weiser, 1969.

Kepler, Johannes. *Harmonice Mandi*. Jena: Diedrich-Verlag, 1969.

Haber, Bruno and Louise. *Man and his World*. York Beach, Maine: Samuel Weiser, Inc., 1978.

———*Life clock in the Horoscope*. York Beach, Maine: Samuel Weiser, Inc., 1982.

BIBLIOGRAPHY